D0057877

I Am Nujood,
Age 10 and Divorced

I Am Nujood,
Age 10 and Divorced

NUJOOD ALI

with DELPHINE MINOUI

Translated by Linda Coverdale

BROADWAY PAPERBACKS
NEW YORK

BROADWAY

English translation copyright © 2010 by Nujood Ali and Delphine Minoui

Reading Group Guide copyright © 2010 by Random House, Inc.

All right reserved.
Published in the United States by Broadway Paperbacks, an imprint of the
Crown Publishing Group, a division of Random House, Inc., New York.
www.crownpublishing.com

Broadway Paperbacks and its logo, a letter B bisected on the diagonal, are
trademarks of Random House, Inc.

Originally published in France as *Moi Nojoud, 10 Ans, Divorcée* by Michel Lafon
Publishing, Paris, in 2009. Copyright © 2009 by Éditions Michel Lafon.
Subsequently published in the United States by Three Rivers Press, an imprint
of the Crown Publishing Group, a division of Random House, Inc., New York,
in 2010.

Library of Congress Cataloging-in-Publication Data
Ali, Nujood.
[Moi Nojoud, 10 ans, divorcée. English]
I am Nujood, age 10 and divorced / Nujood Ali, with Delphine Minoui ;
translated by Linda Coverdale. — 1st ed.
p. cm.
Includes bibliographical references.
1. Child marriage—Yemen (Republic). 2. Ali, Nujood. 3. Girls—Yemen
(Republic)—Social conditions. 4. Yemen (Republic)—Social life and customs.
I. Minoui, Delphine. II. Title.
HQ784.C55A45 2010
306.872'3092—dc22
[B]
2009033063

ISBN 978-0-307-58967-5

Printed in the United States of America

Design by Lauren Dong

18 19 17

First Broadway Paperbacks Edition

Contents

Nujood, a Modern-Day Heroine

Once upon a time there was a magical land with legends as astonishing as its houses, which are adorned with such delicate tracery that they look like gingerbread cottages trimmed with icing. A land at the southernmost tip of the Arabian Peninsula, washed by the Red Sea and the Indian Ocean. A land steeped in a thousand years of history, where adobe turrets perch on the peaks of serried mountains. A land where the scent of incense wafts gaily around the corners of the narrow cobblestone streets.

This country is called Yemen.

But a very long time ago, grown-ups gave it another name: *Arabia Felix*, Happy Arabia.

For Yemen inspires dreams. It is the realm of the Queen of Sheba, an incredibly strong and beautiful woman who inflamed the heart of King Solomon and left her mark in the sacred pages of the Bible and the Koran. It is a mysterious place where men never appear in public without curved daggers worn proudly at their waists, while women hide their charms behind thick black veils.

It is a land that lies along an ancient trade route, a country crossed by merchant caravans laden with fine fabrics, cinnamon, and other aromatic spices. These caravans journeyed on for weeks, sometimes months, never stopping, persevering through wind and rain, and the weakest travelers, the stories say, never came home again.

To see Yemen in your mind's eye, imagine a country a little larger than Syria, Greece, and Nepal all rolled into one, and diving headlong into the Gulf of Aden. Out there, in those tempestuous seas, pirates from many lands lie in wait for merchant ships plying their trades in India, Africa, Europe, and America.

In centuries past, many invaders succumbed to the temptation to claim this lovely land for themselves. Ethiopians came ashore armed with their bows and arrows, but were swiftly driven away. Next came the Persians, with their bushy eyebrows, who constructed canals and fortresses and recruited various native tribes to fight off other invaders. The Portuguese then tried their luck, and set up trading outposts. The Ottomans, who later took up the challenge, held sway in the country for more than a hundred years.

Still later, the British, with their white skin, put into port in the south, in Aden, while the Turks set up shop in the north. And then, once the English were gone, Russians from colder climes set their sights upon the south. Like a cake fought over by greedy children, the country gradually split in two.

Grown-ups say that this *Arabia Felix* has always been the object of envious desire because of its thousand and one treasures. Foreigners covet its oil; its honey is worth its weight in gold; the music of Yemen is captivating, its poetry gentle and refined, its spicy cuisine endlessly pleasing. From around the world, archeologists come to this country to study the architecture of its ruins.

It has been years and years now since the invaders packed up their bags and left, but ever since their departure, Yemen has experienced a series of civil wars too complicated for the pages of children's books. Unified in 1990, the nation still suffers from the wounds left by these many conflicts, like a sick old man, trying to get well, who has lost his bearings and must learn to walk again. Sometimes you even wonder who makes the law in this strange land, where many girls and boys beg in the streets instead of going to school.

Yemen's head of state is a president whose photograph often decorates the display windows of shops, but power in this country lies also with tribal chiefs in turbans who wield enormous authority in the villages, whether it's a question of arms sales, marriage, or the commerce and culture of khat. Then there are those explosions in the capital, Sana'a, in the chic neighborhoods where the diplomatic representatives of foreign nations live, people who drive big cars with tinted windows. And in Yemeni homes, of course, the real law is laid down by fathers and older brothers.

It was in this extraordinary and turbulent country, barely ten years ago, that a little girl named Nujood was born.

A tiny wisp of a thing, Nujood is neither a queen nor a princess. She is a normal girl with parents and plenty of brothers and sisters. Like all children her age, she loves to play hide-and-seek and adores chocolate. She likes to make colored drawings and fantasizes about being a sea turtle, because she has never seen the ocean. When she smiles, a tiny dimple appears in her left cheek.

One cold and gray February evening in 2008, however, that appealing and mischievous grin suddenly melted into bitter tears when her father told her that she was going to wed a man three times her age. It was as if the whole world had landed on her shoulders. Hastily married off a few days later, the little girl resolved to gather all her strength and try to escape her miserable fate. . . .

DELPHINE MINOUI

1

In Court

April 2, 2008

My head is spinning—I've never seen so many people in my whole life. In the yard outside the courthouse, a crowd is bustling around in every direction: men in suits and ties with bunches of yellowed files tucked under their arms; other men wearing the *zanna*, the traditional ankle-length tunic of the villages of northern Yemen; and then all these women, shouting and weeping so loudly that I can't understand a word.

I'd love to read their lips to find out what they're saying, but the *niqab*s that match their long black robes hide everything except their big, round eyes. The women seem furious, as if a tornado had just destroyed their houses. I try to listen closely.

I can catch only a few words—*childcare, justice, human rights*—and I'm not really sure what they mean. Not far away from me is a broad-shouldered giant wearing his turban jammed down to his eyes; he's carrying a plastic bag full of documents and telling anyone who will listen that he has come here to try to get back some land that was stolen from him. He's dashing around like a frantic rabbit, and he almost runs right into me.

What chaos . . . It must be like Al-Qa Square, the one in the heart of Sana'a where out-of-work laborers go, the place Aba—Papa—often talks about. There it's every man for himself, and they all want to be the first to snag a job for the day at dawn, just after the first *azaan*, the traditional summons to prayer called out five times a day by the muezzins from the minarets of their mosques. Poor people are so hungry they've got stones where their hearts should be, and no time to feel pity for the fates of others. Still, I'd like so much for someone here to take my hand, to look at me with kindness. Won't anyone listen to me, for once? It's as if I were invisible. No one sees me: I'm too small for them; I barely come up to their tummies. I'm only ten years old, maybe not even that. Who knows?

I'd imagined the courthouse differently: a calm, clean place, the great house where Good battles Evil, where you can fix all the problems of the world. I'd already seen some courtrooms on my neighbors' television, with judges in long robes. People say they're the ones who can help people in need. So I have to find one and tell him my story. I'm exhausted. It's hot under my veil, I have a headache, and I'm so ashamed. . . . Am I strong enough to keep going? No. Yes. Maybe. . . . I tell myself it's too late to turn back; the hardest part is over, and I have to go on.

When I left my parents' house early this morning, I promised myself not to set foot there again until I'd gotten what I wanted.

"Off you go—buy some bread for breakfast," my mother told me, giving me 150 Yemeni rials, worth about 75 cents.

As a matter of course, I pinned up my long, curly brown hair under my black head scarf and covered my body with a black coat, which is what all Yemeni women wear out in public. Trembling, feeling faint, I walked only a short way before catching the first minibus that passed along the wide avenue leading into town, where I got off at the end of the line. Then, in spite of my fear, for the first time in my life I climbed all alone into a yellow taxi.

Now this endless waiting in the courtyard. To whom should I speak? Unexpectedly, over by the steps leading up to the entrance hall of the big concrete building, I spot what look like a few friendly faces in the crowd: their cheeks dark with dust, three boys in plastic sandals are studying me carefully. They remind me of my little brothers.

"Your weight, ten rials!" one of them calls out to me, shaking a battered old scale.

"Some refreshing tea?" asks another, holding up a small basket full of steaming glasses.

"Fresh carrot juice?" suggests the third boy, breaking into his nicest smile as he stretches out his right hand in the hope of earning a small coin.

No thanks, I'm not thirsty, and what's on my mind has nothing to do with how much I weigh. If they only knew what brings me here . . .

Bewildered, helpless, I look up again into the faces of the many grown-ups hurrying past me. In their long veils, the women all look the same. What kind of a mess have I gotten myself into?

Then I notice a man in a white shirt and black suit walking toward me. A judge, perhaps, or a lawyer? Well, it's an opportunity, so here goes.

"Excuse me, mister, I want to see the judge."

"The judge? Over that way, up the steps," he replies, with hardly a glance at me, before vanishing back into the throng.

I have no choice anymore: I must tackle the staircase now looming before me; it's my last and only chance to get help. I feel dirty and ashamed, but I have to climb these steps, one by one, to go tell my story, to wade through this human flood that grows even bigger the closer I get to the vast entrance hall. I almost fall down, but I catch myself. I've cried so much that my eyes are dry. I'm tired. My feet feel like lead when I finally step onto the marble floor. But I mustn't collapse, not now.

On the white walls, like the ones in a hospital, I can see writing in Arabic, but no matter how I try, I can't manage to read the inscriptions. I was forced to leave school during my second year, right before my life became a nightmare, and aside from my first name, Nujood, I can't write much, which really embarrasses me.

Looking around, I spy a group of men in olive-green uniforms and kepis. They must be policemen, or else soldiers; one of them has a Kalashnikov slung over his shoulder. I'm shaking—if they see me, they might arrest me. A little girl running away from home, that just isn't done. Trembling, I discreetly latch on to the first passing veil, hoping to get the attention of the unknown woman it conceals. A tiny voice inside me whispers, *Go on, Nujood! It's true you're only a girl, but you're also a woman, and a real one, even though you're still having trouble accepting that.*

"I want to talk to the judge."

Two big eyes framed in black stare at me in surprise; the lady in front of me hadn't seen me approach her.

"What?"

"I want to talk to the judge."

Is she not understanding me on purpose, so she can ignore me more easily, like the others?

"Which judge are you looking for?"

"I just want to speak to a judge, that's all!"

"But there are lots of judges in this courthouse."

"Take me to a judge—it doesn't matter which one!"

She stares at me in silence, astonished by my determination. Unless it's my shrill little cry that has frozen her solid.

I'm a simple village girl whose family had to move to the capital, and I have always obeyed the orders of my father and brothers. Since forever, I have learned to say yes to everything.

Today I have decided to say no.

Inside of me I have been soiled, contaminated— it's as if part of myself has been stolen from me. No one has the right to keep me from seeking justice. It's my last chance, so I'm not going to give up easily. And this surprised stare, which feels as cold as the marble of the great hall where my cry now echoes strangely, will not make me keep quiet. It's almost noon; I've been wandering desperately in this labyrinth of a courthouse for hours. I want to see the judge!

"Follow me," the woman finally says, gesturing for me to walk along behind her.

The door opens onto a room with brown carpeting. It's full of people, and at the far end, behind a desk, a thin-faced man with a mustache busily replies to the barrage of questions coming at him from all directions. It's the judge, at last.

The atmosphere is noisy, but reassuring. I feel safe. I recognize, in a place of honor on a wall, a framed photograph of Amm Ali, "Uncle Ali": that's what I've been taught in school to call the president of our country, Ali Abdullah al-Saleh, who was elected more than thirty years ago.

Outside, the muezzin issues the midday call to prayer as I sit down, like everyone else, in one of the brown armchairs lined up along the wall. Around me I catch glimpses of familiar faces—or, rather, familiar eyes—from the angry crowd in the courtyard. Certain faces lean toward me in a strange way. They've finally realized that I exist! It's about time. Comforted, I rest my head against the back of the chair and patiently await my turn.

If God exists, I say to myself, *then let Him come save me.* I have always recited the five required daily prayers. During Eid al-Fitr, when we celebrate the end of Ramadan, the Islamic holy month of fasting, I dutifully help my mother and sisters with all the cooking. I'm basically a very good girl. *Oh, God, have pity on me!* My mind is dizzy with images that come and go. . . . I'm swimming; the sea is calm. Then the water becomes choppy. I catch sight of my brother Fares off in the distance, but I can't go to him. When I call to him, he doesn't hear me, so I begin shouting his name. Then gusts of wind blow me backward toward the shore. I struggle, whirling my hands around like propellers—I'm not going to let myself be driven all the way back to where I started, but I'm so close to the shore now, and I've lost sight of Fares. . . . Help! I don't want to go back to Khardji, no, I don't want to go back there!

"And what can I do for you?"

A man's voice rouses me from my dozing. It is a curiously gentle voice, with no need to be loud to attract my attention, simply whispering a few words: "And what can I do for you?" At last someone has come to my rescue. I rub my face and recognize, standing tall there in front of me, the judge with the mustache. The crowd has gone, the eyes have disappeared, and the room is almost empty. I have not replied, so the man tries again.

"What do you want?"

This time I answer promptly.

"I want a divorce!"

2

Khardji

In Khardji, the village where I was born, women are not taught how to make choices. When she was about sixteen, Shoya, my mother, married my father, Ali Mohammad al-Ahdel, without a word of protest. And when he decided four years later to enlarge the family by choosing a second wife, my mother obediently accepted his decision.

It was with that same resignation that I at first agreed to my marriage, without realizing what was at stake. At my age, you don't ask yourself many questions.

One day, in all innocence, I had asked Omma—Mama—a question.

"How are babies made?"

"You'll find out when you're older," she'd replied, sweeping away my question with a wave of her hand.

So I'd simply put my childish curiosity back in the

cupboard and gone out to play in the garden with my brothers and sisters. Our favorite game was hide-and-seek, and the valley of Wadi La'a, in the northern Yemeni province of Hajja, offered a wealth of hiding places where we could easily conceal ourselves: tree trunks, big rocks, caves carved out by time. When we were breathless from too much running around, we'd dive into the cool grass to be soothed by our little nests of greenery, where the sun caressed our skin and tanned our already dusky cheeks. Rested and refreshed, we'd amuse ourselves further by chasing the chickens and teasing the donkeys with sticks.

My mother bore sixteen children. For her, each pregnancy was a real challenge. She mourned three miscarriages in silence, and she lost one of her babies at birth. And because there was no doctor, four of my brothers and sisters, whom I never knew, died of illness between the ages of two months and four years.

Omma gave birth to me the way she delivered all her children: at home, lying on a woven mat, sweating, suffering terribly, and begging God to protect her newborn.

Now and then, to satisfy my curiosity, she would speak to me of my arrival.

"You were a long time coming out. The contractions began in the middle of the night, at around two in the morning. And the birth lasted a good half day, in midsummer, in withering heat. It was a Friday, a holy day."

But even if I'd been born on an ordinary weekday, it wouldn't have made much difference. There was never any question of Omma giving birth in a hospital. Our village was all the way at the end of the valley, far from any medical facilities, and Khardji was only five little stone houses without any grocery store, garage, barber, city hall, or even a mosque. There was no way to get there except by mule. Only a few brave pickup drivers dared take the rocky path along the edge of the ravine, a road so bad they had to change their tires every two months. So imagine the scene if my mother had chosen to go to the hospital: she would have given birth right out in the open! Omma says that even the mobile medical clinics never risked trying to reach Khardji.

Whenever she was worn out by my questions and forgot to tell me the end of my story, I would spur Omma on.

"But then who acted as nurse in our house?"

"Well, luckily, your big sister Jamila was there. As always, she was the one who helped me cut the cord, with a kitchen knife. Then she gave you your first bath, before wrapping you in a cloth. Nujood is a

Bedouin name, people say, and it was your grandfather Jad who gave it to you."

"Omma, was I born in June or July? Or right in the middle of August?"

This is the point at which Omma usually begins to get testy.

"Nujood, when are you going to stop pestering me like this?"

And that puts an end to my questions.

Actually, she stops answering me because she doesn't know what to say, since my name does not appear in any way in the official registers. Out in the countryside, people have bushels of babies without bothering with identity cards. As for the year of my birth, who knows? By deduction, my mother says today that I must be around ten, but I could just as well be eight or nine. Sometimes, when I'm persistent, Omma undertakes a careful calculation to try to establish the birth order of her children. For her reference points she uses the seasons, the deaths of relatives, the marriages of certain cousins, the times we moved house, and so on. It's a real feat of mental acrobatics.

And so, after an accounting much more complicated than when she goes to the corner grocery store in Sana'a, she deduces each time that Jamila is the oldest child, followed by Mohammad, the first boy (and "second man" of the family, the one who has the power of decision right after my father). Next are Mona the mysterious and Fares the impetuous. And then me, followed by my "pet" sister, Haïfa, who's almost as tall as I am. Finally, Morad, Abdo, Assil, Khaled, and the last little girl, Rawdha with the curly hair. As for Dowla, my "aunt" (and my father's second wife, who is also one of his distant cousins), she has five children.

"Omma's a good laying hen," Mona often says with a laugh when she feels like teasing our mother, and I remember waking up more than once in the morning to find a newborn baby in Omma's bed for her to cluck over. She'll never stop.

Omma does remember, however, being visited once by the representative of an association called "family planning." They gave her a prescription for tablets to keep her from getting pregnant, and she took them from time to time, on days when she remembered them. One month later, though, to her great surprise, her belly began to swell again, and she decided that such was life: sometimes you cannot go against nature.

❧

Khardji is well named. In Arabic, *khardji* means "outside"—in other words, at the ends of the earth. Most geographers don't even take the trouble to put this microscopic place on any maps. Let's just say that Khardji is not too far from Hajja, an important city in northwestern Yemen, to the north of Sana'a. Traveling between this tiny lost locality and the capital requires at least four hours on paved road, and the same again over sand and rubble. When my brothers used to set out in the morning for classes, they walked for a good two hours to reach the school, which was in a larger village in the valley. School was reserved for them, since my father, a very protective man, considered girls too fragile and vulnerable to venture out alone on those almost deserted paths where danger lurked behind every cactus. Besides, neither he nor my mother knew how to read or write, so they didn't really see any need for their girls to learn, either. Out in the countryside, most of the women are illiterate.

So I grew up in the school of the great outdoors, watching Omma take care of the house and itching for the day I would be old enough to tag along with my two big sisters, Jamila and Mona, when they left to fetch water from the spring in little yellow jerry cans. The climate in Yemen is so dry that everyone must drink several liters of water every day to avoid dehydration. As soon as I learned to walk, the river became one of my chief haunts. It flowed past only a few yards below the house, and was quite useful to us: Omma did our laundry there, and rinsed out the cooking pots after every meal in its clear waters. After the men left for the fields in the morning, the women went to the river to wash in the shade of the tall trees. On stormy days, we'd take refuge at home from the lightning and rain, but as soon as the sun's rays broke through the clouds again, we children would dash back to the river, now swollen with water that came up to my neck. To keep its banks from overflowing, my brothers would build little dikes to channel its current.

On their way home from school, the boys would gather branches to feed the fire for the tandoor, the traditional cylindrical clay oven in which we cooked *khobz*, our Yemeni bread. My older sisters were experts in the preparation of these crusty flatbreads, which we sometimes drizzled with honey, "the gold of Yemen," as the grown-ups say. The honey of our region is especially famous, and my father had several beehives he cared for with astonishing tenderness. Omma never tired of telling us that honey was good for the health and provided energy.

Supper was traditionally eaten around a *sofrah*, a large cloth spread out on the floor, which many Arab

Muslims use instead of a table at mealtime. As soon as Omma had set down the piping-hot stewpot full of *salta*, a spicy ragout of beef or mutton in an aromatic fenugreek sauce, we would plunge in our hands to roll up little balls of rice and meat that swiftly vanished down our throats. By imitating our parents, we learned to eat straight from the serving dishes. No plates, no forks, no knives: that's how we eat in the villages of Yemen.

Now and then Omma would take us to the market held every Saturday in the heart of the valley, and for us, this was a major excursion. We'd go there on donkeys to stock up on provisions. If the sun beat down too harshly, Omma would wear a straw hat over the black veil that covered a good part of her face. She looked like a sunflower!

We were living rather happily, to the rhythm of the sun. It was a simple life, but peaceful, without electricity or running water. Off behind a bush, the toilet was just a hole within low brick walls. Decorated modestly with a few cushions lying on the floor, the main room of our home turned into a bedroom at night. To go from one room to another, we had to cross the central courtyard, which became our living room in the summer, adapting itself to all our family's needs. Omma would set up an outdoor kitchen there, simmering *salta*s on the wood fire while she nursed the youngest children. My brothers would study the alphabet out in the fresh air. We girls would take naps on a mattress of straw.

My father was not often at home. He usually rose at first light to take his animals out to graze. He had eighty sheep and four cows, which gave us enough milk to make butter, yogurt, and soft white cheese. Whenever he went to visit our next-door neighbors, he always wore a brown jacket over his *zanna* and a ceremonial dagger called a *jambia* at his belt. The men of my country all wear this sharp, hand-decorated dagger, which is said to be a symbol of authority, manhood, and prestige in Yemeni society. And it's true that it gave our father a certain self-assurance, a noticeable dash of style. I was proud of my Aba. But as I understand it, these weapons are more than simple decoration, since everyone wants to be the one wearing the handsomest *jambia*. And their cost varies, depending on whether the handle is made of plastic, ivory, or real rhinoceros horn. According to the codes of our tribal culture, it is forbidden to use these daggers in self-defense or to attack an adversary during an argument. On the contrary: the *jambia* may be used to help resolve conflicts and is, above all, a symbol of tribal justice. My father would never have imagined he would ever need his, until that unlucky day when we were forced to flee our village within twenty-four hours.

I was between two and three years old when the scandal broke out. The circumstances were most unusual: Omma was in the capital, Sana'a, for health problems, and for reasons surely related to her absence—the details of which were unknown to me at the time—a violent dispute broke out between my father and the other villagers in Khardji. During the arguments, my sister Mona's name kept coming up. It was then decided to resolve the conflict in the tribal manner, by placing *jambia*s and bundles of rial notes between the protagonists, but the discussion degenerated and, in an exceptional breach of protocol, blades were drawn. The other villagers accused my family of having trampled the honor of Khardji and stained its reputation. My father was beside himself. He felt swindled, demeaned by those he had thought were his friends. All I knew was that Mona, the second daughter of our family and thirteen years old at most, had suddenly gotten married. What, exactly, had happened? I was too little to understand. One day, I would find out, but at the time I knew only that we had to leave right away—and leave everything behind: sheep, cows, chickens, bees, and our memories of what I had thought was a small corner of paradise.

Our arrival in Sana'a was quite a shock. The capital was a blur of dust and noise that was hard to get used to.

The contrast between the green Wadi La'a valley and the barrenness of the sprawling city was brutal, because outside the ancient heart of the city, with its lovely traditional adobe houses, their windows outlined in lacy white designs, the urban landscape becomes a vulgar confusion of dismal concrete buildings. Out in the street, I was exactly on a level with all the exhaust pipes belching diesel fumes, which made my throat sore. There were hardly any parks where we children could run and play, and you had to buy tickets to most of the amusement parks, so only rich people went there.

We moved into the ground floor of a slum building on a garbage-strewn alley in the neighborhood of Al-Qa. Aba was depressed. He hardly spoke. He had lost his appetite. How could a simple illiterate peasant without a diploma hope to support his family in this capital, already collapsing under its burden of unemployed people? Other villagers had already come to seek their fortunes here only to run into a wall of problems. Some men had been reduced to sending their wives and children to beg for coins in public squares. By knocking on doors, my father finally landed a job as a sweeper for the local sanitation authority, at a salary that barely paid our rent, and whenever we were late with that, our landlord would shout angrily at us. Omma would weep, and no one could sweeten her sadness.

When he was twelve years old, Fares, the fourth child in the family, began to want the things all boys long for at his age. Every day he'd demand money to go buy himself candies, stylish trousers, and new shoes like the ones we saw in billboard advertisements. Beautiful, brand-new shoes that would have cost our father more than a month's salary! Jolly and rambunctious by nature, Fares kept demanding more and more, and even began to threaten my parents, telling them he would run away if they didn't manage to satisfy his cravings. He was a show-off, true, but he was still my favorite brother. At least he didn't hit me like Mohammad, my eldest brother, who acted like the head of the family. I admired Fares for his ambition, his energy, his way of standing up to everyone without worrying about their reactions. He made choices and stuck to them, even if he had to take on the entire family. One day, after an argument with our father, he left the house and did not come back.

For the first time in my life, I saw Aba cry. To drown his sorrow, he began going off for long hours to chew khat with some old acquaintances, and wound up losing his job. Omma started having bad dreams, and in the main room where we children slept by her side on little mattresses laid on the floor, I was awakened several times in the middle of the night by her sobbing. She was suffering, and it showed.

Fares had gone without leaving a trace, except for one tiny thing: an identity photo, in color, which Mohammad kept carefully in the deepest part of his wallet. No doubt about it—it was Fares in the snapshot: with head held high, a white turban planted on his curly brown hair (to make him look "grown-up," no doubt), he stared right at the camera with a naughty, twinkling eye.

And then, two years after his flight, we received an unexpected phone call, the first sign of life.

"Saudi Arabia," we heard at the other end of the line. "Everything's fine. . . . Shepherd, I'm working as a shepherd. . . . Don't worry about me. . . ."

His voice had changed—he sounded more confident—but I recognized him right away. But the line, crackling with static, quickly went dead. How had Fares wound up so far away? What city was he actually in? Had he been lucky enough to take a plane, flying up into the clouds? And exactly where was Saudi Arabia, anyway? Was there any seashore where he was? I had so many questions. I overheard Aba, Omma, and Mohammad speculating that Fares had been the object of child trafficking, which is supposedly rather frequent in Yemen. Did that mean he had found some adoptive parents? Perhaps he was happy after all, and could finally buy himself the candy and blue jeans he wanted so much. As for me, I missed him terribly.

To help me forget his loss, I withdrew into my dreams. Dreams of water—not of rivers, but the ocean. I've always wanted to be like a sea turtle so that I could stick my head underwater. I have never seen the sea. With my colored pencils, I would draw waves in my little notebook. I imagined they were green or blue.

"They're blue," my girlfriend Malak informed me one day, looking over my shoulder.

Malak and I had become inseparable. I had met her in the Al-Qa neighborhood school, where my parents had finally agreed to register me. During recess, we often played marbles. Out of the seventy pupils—all girls—crammed into the classroom, she was my best friend. I'd done very well there my first year, and had just begun my second. Malak would stop by in the morning to get me and we'd go off to school together.

"Blue? How would you know?" I asked her.

"For vacation my parents take me to Al-Hudaydah. It's by the Red Sea."

"What does the water taste like?"

"It's salty."

"And the sand—it's blue, too?"

"No, it's yellow, and it's so, so soft, if you only knew. . . ."

"And what's in the sea?"

"Boats, fish, and people swimming."

Malak told me that she'd learned to swim there. I had never even dipped my toe into a kiddie pool, so I was fascinated. No matter how hard I tried to understand how she managed to stay on the surface of the water, I could never figure out that mystery. All I remembered is that in Khardji, Omma would always shout a warning at me when I went too near the river: "Watch out—if you fall in, you'll sink!"

Malak said that her mother had bought her a bathing suit in pretty colors, and that she herself could even build sand castles with turrets and grand staircases that then melted away into the waves. One day she held a big shell she'd brought back from Al-Hudaydah up against my ear.

"Listen, and you'll hear the sea."

"The waves, oh, I hear the waves!" I yelped. "It's unbelievable!"

To me, water was, above all, rain, which is becoming very scarce in Yemen. Sometimes we would be startled by hail in the middle of summertime. What happiness! We children would dash into the street to collect the little hailstones in a basin. I'd count them proudly, because at school I had learned to count from one to a hundred. When the ice had melted, we'd have fun sprinkling the cold water onto our faces to cool off. Mona had been fairly glum since coming to live with us in Sana'a two months after our hasty departure from Khardji, but even she would sometimes join us in our revelry after those extraordinary hailstorms.

Mona had arrived with the husband who had so suddenly imposed himself on her life, and as the years went by, she gradually recovered her natural smile, her mocking air, and the sense of humor that so often exasperated Omma. Mona brought two pretty babies into the world, Monira and Nasser, who filled her with joy. Our family and her husband's wound up growing closer, and to reinforce this union, they talked about marrying my big brother Mohammad to one of his brother-in-law's sisters, following the tradition of *sighar*.

But it was too good to last. One day, Mona's husband vanished from the scene, and so did my big sister Jamila. Had they, like Fares, run away in the hope of making their fortune in Saudi Arabia, and perhaps bringing us back some electronic toys or a color television? In my parents' room, there was much whispering about the two of them, but we children were strictly forbidden to ask any questions. I remember only that right after their mysterious disappearance, which I would come to understand only much later, Mona became capricious and moody again. Most of the time she was melancholy and depressed; then, all of a sudden, she would burst into laughter that would revive her natural beauty, enhancing her big brown eyes and delicate features. Mona really possessed lots of charm.

Whether she was having a good day or a bad one, though, Mona was always particularly sweet to me, even protective—sort of a maternal instinct. Sometimes she'd take me with her to window-shop on Hayle Avenue, famous for its clothing stores. Gazing enviously at the window displays, I admired the sequined evening gowns, the red skirts, the silk blouses in blue, violet, yellow, and green. I imagined that I was changed into a princess. There were even wedding dresses, which looked like movie costumes or magical fairy-tale gowns. So beautiful. The stuff of dreams.

One February evening in 2008, when I'd just gotten home, Aba told me he had some good news.

"Nujood, you are about to be married."

3

The Judge

Judge Abdo cannot conceal his surprise.

"You want a divorce?"

"Yes."

"But . . . you mean you're married?"

"Yes!"

His features are distinguished. His white shirt sets off his olive skin. But when he hears my reply, his face darknes. He seems to have trouble believing me.

"At your age? How can you already be married?"

Without bothering to answer his question, I repeat in a determined voice: "I want a divorce."

I don't sob, not even once, while speaking to him. I feel trembly, but I know what I want: I want an end to this hell. I've had enough of suffering in silence.

"But you're so young and frail," he murmurs.

I look at him and nod. He starts nervously scratching his mustache. If only he'll agree to save me! He's a judge, after all. He must have lots of power.

"And why do you want a divorce?" he continues in a more natural tone, as if trying to hide his aston-ishment.

I look him straight in the eye. "Because my hus-band beats me."

It's as if I had slapped him right in the face. His expression freezes again. He has just realized that something serious has happened to me and that I have no reason to lie to him. Point-blank, he asks me an important question: "Are you still a virgin?"

· I swallow hard. I'm ashamed of talking about these things. It's deeply upsetting. In my country, women must keep their distance from men they don't know. And this is the first time I've ever seen this judge. But in that same instant I understand that if I want to win, I must take the plunge.

"No. I bled."

He's shocked. Abruptly, I have the feeling that of the two of us, he is the one who's flinching. I can see his surprise, see him trying to conceal his emotions. Then he takes a deep breath and says, "I'm going to help you."

I feel strangely relieved, actually, to have been able to confide in someone at last. My body feels so much lighter. I watch him grab his phone with a shaking hand. I hear him say a few things to someone who must be a colleague of his. As he talks, he waves his other hand all around. He appears determined to try to rescue me from my misery. If only he can solve the problem once and for all! With a bit of luck, he'll act quickly, very quickly, and this evening I'll be able to go home to my parents and play with my brothers and sisters, just like before. In a few hours, I will be divorced. Divorced! Free again. Without a husband, without that dread of finding myself alone, at nightfall, in the same bedroom with *him*. Without that fear of suffering, over and over, that same torment.

I am celebrating too soon.

A second judge joins us in the room, and he dashes my enthusiasm to bits.

"My child, this might very well take a lot more time than you think. It's a delicate and difficult case. And unfortunately, I cannot promise that you will win."

This second man is named Mohammad al-Ghazi, and according to Abdo, he's the chief judge. Mohammad al-Ghazi seems embarrassed, ill at ease. In his entire career, he says, he has never seen a case like mine. They both explain to me that in Yemen girls are frequently married off quite young, before the legal age of fifteen. An ancient tradition, adds Judge Abdo. But to his knowledge, none of these precocious marriages has ever ended in divorce—because no little girl has, until now, showed up at a courthouse. A question of family honor, it seems. My situation is most exceptional, and complicated.

"We'll have to find a lawyer," Abdo explains, somewhat at a loss.

A lawyer—but what for? Of what use is a court if it can't even grant divorces on the spot? I couldn't care less about being an exceptional case. Laws are for helping people, yes or no? These judges seem very nice, but do they realize that if I go home without any guarantee, my husband will come get me and the torture will start all over again? No, I don't want to go home.

"I want to get divorced!"

I frown fiercely to show I mean it.

The sound of my own voice makes me jump. I must have raised my voice too loud—or is it these big white walls that make everything echo?

"We'll find a solution, we'll find a solution," Mohammad al-Ghazi murmurs, straightening his turban.

But he has more than one cause for concern: the clock has just struck two in the afternoon, when offices close. Today is Wednesday, and the Muslim weekend is about to begin. The courthouse will not re-open before Saturday. I realize that they, too, are worried about my going back home, after what they've just heard.

"It's out of the question, her going home. And who knows what might happen to her if she wanders the streets alone," continues Mohammad al-Ghazi.

Abdo has an idea: Why couldn't I take refuge at his house? He still can't get over my story and is willing to do anything to tear me from the grip of my husband. But he must quickly withdraw his offer when he remembers that his wife and children have gone to the country for a few days, leaving him on his own. Our Islamic traditions stipulate that a woman must not be left alone with a man who is not her *mahram*, her close blood relative.

What to do?

A third judge, Abdel Wahed, finally volunteers his help. His family is at home, and they have room to take me in. I'm saved, at least for the moment. He, too, has a mustache, but he is more stocky than Abdo. His wire-rimmed glasses make him look very serious, and he's quite imposing in his suit. I hardly dare speak to him. But I pull myself together; it's better to overcome my shyness than to go home. And besides, what reassures me is that he seems like a real papa, who takes good care of his children. Not like mine.

His big car is comfortable and perfectly clean. There is even cool air coming out of little vents, which tickles my face. It's nice. I barely open my mouth during the ride. I'm not sure whether it's from timidity, uneasiness, or because, finally, I feel all right with these grown-ups taking care of me.

"You're a very brave girl," says Abdel Wahed, breaking the silence. "Bravo! Don't worry—you have the right to demand a divorce. Other girls before you have had the same problems, but unfortunately they didn't dare talk about them. We'll do everything we can to protect you. And we will never allow you to be sent back to your husband, never. That's a promise."

My lips curve into a little crescent moon. It's been so long since I smiled.

"Perhaps you don't realize it yet," adds the judge, "but you're an exceptional girl."

I blush.

When we arrive at his house, Abdel Wahed hurries to introduce me to his wife, Saba, and to his children. Shima, their daughter, must be three or four years younger than I am. In her bedroom she has lots of

Fulla dolls, a Middle Eastern version of the American Barbie with blond hair that all the little girls in Yemen dream about.

"You poor thing," says Shima. "*Haram!* It's not fair!"

In Islam, anything forbidden and punishable by divine law is *haram*, so the child's indignant reaction is only natural: Shima's mother has explained to her that a bad man has beaten me. Shima frowns, imitating an adult scolding someone. I'm touched by her sympathy. With a smile of complicity, she motions for me to come away and play with her, then takes me by the hand.

As for the four boys, they're busy watching cartoons. There are two televisions in this house—what luxury!

"Please feel right at home," Saba says to me in a soft and welcoming voice.

So this is what family life is. I'd been so scared that I would seem like a freak to them, but they have quickly adopted me, and I am quite at ease. They make me feel that I can tell them everything without being judged. Without being punished. That evening, sitting cross-legged in the living room, is the first time that I have the strength to tell my story.

4

The Wedding

February 2008

With Mona, I'd lose all track of time while strolling along Hayle Avenue. Sometimes we pressed our noses so long against the front window of our favorite shop that the evening clothes disappeared behind the steamed-up glass. The white wedding dress on a plastic mannequin always caught my fancy. A dress for a lady! And what a contrast with all those women in the street, draped from head to toe in black.

"*Insha'Allah,* God willing, you'll have one like this the day of your wedding," Mona would whisper, her sparkling eyes framed by the *niqab* that covered the rest of her face whenever she left the house.

Mona rarely smiled. Fate had not smiled on her with a joyous wedding. Married in a hurry, she'd had to make do with a blue dress, and aside from that detail, she was always evasive about the circumstances of her marriage. Ever since her husband had abruptly disappeared to who knows where, it had become a closed subject. I imagined he was traveling some-where, far away from Yemen, but I was careful not to ask a single question. If I did, Mona would simply murmur that all she wanted for me was that I be happy and wind up with an affectionate and respect-ful husband.

I would never have imagined that my wedding day would arrive so quickly.

And anyway, I didn't have a really clear idea of what marriage was. To me, it was a big celebration most of all, with lots of presents, and chocolate, and jewelry. A new house, a new life! A few years earlier, I'd attended various celebrations held for some dis-tant boy and girl cousins, where there was music and dancing. Beneath their *baltos*, their long black coats, the women were elegantly dressed. Their faces were exquisitely made up, their tresses smoothed by the hairdresser, like the pictures on bottles of shampoo, with little butterfly barrettes in the bangs of the most coquettish girls. I always had great fun at those parties. I remember the henna decorations on the hands and arms of the young brides, with designs like flowers. It was so beautiful, the henna. And I would think, *One day I'll have henna on my hands, too.*

The Wedding

❧

The news came out of nowhere. When Aba informed me that my turn had come, I didn't really understand. At first I felt almost relieved, as if marriage were an escape hatch, because life at home had become impossible. Aba had never been able to find full-time employment after losing his street-sweeper job, so we were always late with the rent, and the landlord regularly threatened to evict us.

To save money, Omma now cooked only rice and vegetable stews. She had begun teaching me how to help her with the household duties. We baked *shafout*, a kind of large pancake slathered with yogurt flavored with garlic and onion, and *bint al-sahn*, a delicious dessert prepared with honey. When my father brought home enough money, Omma would send one of my brothers out to buy a chicken she would cook for Friday, the Muslim holy day. Red meat? Forget it—too expensive. In fact, I hadn't had any *fatah*, beef stew, since my first-ever meal in a restaurant, where some cousins had invited us to celebrate Eid. We'd even been allowed to drink some "Bebsi," a black soda from America. And when we left the restaurant, a waiter sprinkled the grown-ups' hands with perfume—and mine, too! It smelled wonderful.

Omma had also taught me to bake flatbread. She used to light the fire while I kneaded the dough, which she would then spread into the shape of a full moon before pressing it against the inner wall of the tandoor oven. One day, though, she had to relinquish her tandoor in exchange for a little money on the black market. Each time our purse was empty, she would sell a few of our possessions. Basically, she had given up relying on my father.

And then came the day when there wasn't much left to sell. After they'd missed enough meals for want of money, my brothers finally joined the young street vendors who tap on car windshields at red lights, hoping to trade a packet of facial tissues or some chewing gum for a few coins. Even Mona joined them, but begging played some mean tricks on her. Within twenty-four hours she was picked up by the police and sent off to a detention center. When she returned home, she told us she'd found herself among ladies accused of going with several men at the same time, and that the women guards in the prison pulled everyone's hair. When she had gotten over her fright, she went out again to beg and wound up once more nose to nose with the police. After that second incarceration, she gave up her risky escapades. Then it was Haïfa's and my turn to try it. Hand in hand, we went out to scratch our nails on car windows, barely daring even to glance at the drivers, who quite often ignored us. I didn't like that, but we had no choice.

On days when Aba didn't lie too long in bed, he left home to go crouch on his heels like the other jobless men on one of the public squares in the neighborhood, hoping to land a day's work as a laborer, mason, or handyman for a thousand or so rials—about five dollars. More and more often now, he was spending his afternoons chewing khat with some neighbors. He claimed it helped him forget his troubles, and this routine had become a ritual. Sitting cross-legged with the other local men, he would select the best green leaves from a small plastic bag and tuck them into a corner of his mouth. The emptier the bag became, the more swollen his cheek grew, until the leaves formed a ball he would chew for hours and hours.

It was during one of those khat sessions that a man of about thirty had approached him.

"I would like our two families to be united," the man had said.

His name was Faez Ali Thamer, and he worked as a deliveryman, carrying packages everywhere on his motorcycle. Like us, he was originally from the village of Khardji, and he was looking for a wife. My father accepted his proposal immediately. As the next in line after my two big sisters Jamila and Mona, I was the logical one to be married off. When Aba returned home, his mind was already made up. And no one could change it.

That very evening, I overheard a conversation between Mona and our father.

"Nujood is way too young to get married," Mona insisted.

"Too young? When the prophet Mohammad wed Aïsha, she was only nine years old," replied Aba.

"Yes, but that was in the time of the Prophet. Now things are different."

"Listen—this marriage, it's the best way to protect her."

"What do you mean by that?"

"You know perfectly well. She will be spared the same problems you and Jamila had. This way she won't be raped by a stranger and become the prey of evil rumors. This man seems honest, at least. He's known in the neighborhood. He comes from our village. And he has promised not to touch Nujood until she's older."

"But—"

"I've made my decision! Besides, you know we

haven't enough money to feed the whole family. So this will mean one less mouth."

My mother never said a thing. She seemed sad, but resigned. After all, she had wed through an arranged marriage, like most Yemeni women, so she was in a good position to know that in our country it's the men who give the orders, and the women who follow them. For her to defend me was a waste of time.

I kept hearing my father's words in my mind: *one less mouth*. So that's all I was to him, a burden, and he had seized the first chance to get rid of me. It was true that I hadn't always been the good little girl he would have liked to have, but after all, isn't getting into mischief part of being a child? And I loved him in spite of his faults, and that nasty smell of khat, and his insistence that we go beg for a few crusts of bread in the street.

The same problems you and Jamila had. What did he mean by that? All I knew was that a week had gone by, then another, and another, and Jamila had not come back. Like Mona's husband, she had abruptly vanished. I had even given up keeping track of how many days I had gone without seeing her. She used to visit us so often, and now she had simply disappeared. I was quite fond of Jamila. Every once in a while, she had brought me sweets; although she was shy and not very talkative, she was thoughtful and generous. And Mona's husband had never come back after his mysterious disappearance, either. Where had he gone? Grown-ups and their affairs were too complicated for me.

After her son vanished, Mona's mother-in-law had demanded custody of her grandchildren, three-year-old Monira and eighteen-month-old Nasser. Heartsick, Mona had fought like a tigress to keep her children, and her tenacity had brought her a partial victory: pleading the necessity of nursing her baby son, she managed to hold on to him. Now, haunted by the thought of losing him, she never took her eyes off him. Whenever he wandered off, she ran to catch him up in her arms, holding him tight as if he were a treasure she were trying to hide.

My wedding preparations moved rapidly ahead, and I soon realized my misfortune when my future husband's family decided that I must leave school a month before the wedding night. I hugged Malak sadly, promising her that I would soon be back.

"One day, we'll go together to the seashore," she murmured, holding me close.

That was the last time I ever saw her.

I had to say good-bye as well to my two favorite teachers, Samia and Samira. With them, I had learned to write my first name in Arabic letters, from right to left: the curve of the *noon*, the sway of the *jeem*, the loop of the *wow*, and the pincers of the *del*: Nujood! I owed them so much.

Mathematics and Koran study were two of my favorite subjects. We had memorized the Five Pillars of Islam in class: the *shahada*, or profession of faith; *salat*, prayer for guidance; the *hajj*, the great pilgrimage to Mecca; *zakat*, alms to the poor; and Ramadan, the monthlong fast during which Muslims neither eat nor drink from sunrise to sunset. My classmates and I had promised Samia that when we were older, we would observe Ramadan like the grown-ups did.

My favorite subject, though, was drawing. With my colored pencils I used to draw flowers and pears, and villas with blue roofs, green shutters, and red chimneys. Sometimes I would add a uniformed guard to stand in front of the entrance gate because I'd heard that rich people's houses were protected by guards. I always drew big fruit trees in the garden. Plus a pretty little pond, right in the middle.

During recess we played hide-and-seek and recited nursery rhymes. I loved school. It was my refuge, a happiness all my own.

I also had to give up my escapades at our next-door neighbors' house, only a few yards from ours, where they had a transistor radio. My little sister Haïfa and I had taken to visiting them to listen to tapes by Haïfa Wehbe and Nancy Ajram, two beautiful Lebanese singers with long hair and heavy makeup. They had lovely eyes and perfect noses; we used to imitate them, batting our eyelids and wiggling our hips. We also liked the Yemeni singer Jamila Saad, who was a real star. "You think so much of yourself," she warbled in one of her love songs, "You think you're simply the best."

The people next door were also among the few in the neighborhood lucky enough to have a television. The TV was my ticket to travel. I adored watching *Tom and Jerry*, my favorite cartoon, and a show called *Adnan and Lina*, which told the story of two friends who had met on a far-off island. I think they were supposed to be Japanese, or maybe Chinese, but the amazing thing was that they spoke Arabic, just like me, and without an accent. Adnan was a brave boy who was always ready to save Lina; in fact, he saved her repeatedly from bad people who tried to kidnap her. She was so lucky! I envied her a lot.

Adnan reminded me of Eyman, a young boy from Al-Qa I will never forget. One day when I was walking in the street with some of my girlfriends, a neighborhood boy stopped us and started frightening us, saying nasty things that seemed insulting. He was laughing at our scared expressions when Eyman appeared like magic to challenge him.

"Get out or I'll throw stones in your face!" Eyman told him.

When Eyman's threat finally drove the boy away, it was such a relief. That was the only time anyone had ever come to my defense, and Eyman became my imaginary hero. I told myself that when I was grown up, maybe I'd be lucky enough to have a husband like him.

On my wedding day, my female cousins began to ululate and clap their hands when they caught sight of me arriving. I, however, could hardly see their faces, my eyes were so full of tears. I advanced slowly, doing my best to avoid tripping over my outfit, which was too big for me and dragged on the ground. I'd been hastily dressed in a long tunic of a faded chocolate color, which belonged to the wife of my future brother-in-law. A female relative had taken charge of my hair, which she gathered into a chignon that weighed down my head. I didn't even get to wear any mascara. Catching sight of my face in a small mirror—round cheeks, pink lips, and brown, almond-shaped eyes—I'd noticed how smooth my brow was, and try as I might, I couldn't find a single wrinkle. I was young, too young.

Barely two weeks had passed since I had been spoken for. Following local custom, the women celebrated my wedding in my parents' tiny house; there were forty of us, all told. Meanwhile, the men gathered at the house of one of my uncles to celebrate, and to chew khat yet again. Two days earlier, when the marriage contract had been signed, the event had also been men only, and occurred behind closed doors. Everything had happened without me. Neither my mother, my sisters, nor I had had any right to know how things had gone. We found out the details late that afternoon only through my little brothers, who had gone off to beg a few coins in the street to pay for refreshments for my father, my uncle, and my future husband, along with his father and brother. We learned that the meeting had taken place according to well-established tribal protocol. My father's brother-in-law, the only one present who could read and write, acted as notary, drawing up the marriage contract. My dowry had been set at 150,000 rials, a sum equivalent to 750 dollars.

"Don't worry," I heard my father whisper to my mother that night. "They made him promise not to touch Nujood before the year after she has her first period."

I shuddered.

My wedding celebration, which began at lunchtime, was quickly over. No white dress. No henna flowers on my hands. No coconut candies, my absolute favorites, the ones that hold the sweet taste of happy days. It was over quickly—but to me it seemed to last forever. Sitting in a corner of the room, I refused to dance with the other women because I was gradually realizing that my life was undergoing a complete upheaval, and not for the better. The youngest women began to improvise a belly dance, baring their navels and undulating their bodies like something out of a tacky video. Holding hands, the older women performed more traditional folk dances, like the ones still seen in villages. During lulls in the music, they came over to greet me, and I embraced them dutifully. But I couldn't even pretend to smile.

I just sat impassively in my corner of the main room, my face swollen from crying. I didn't want to leave my family. I didn't feel prepared. I already missed school painfully, and Malak even more. Catching sight of my little sister Haïfa's sad face during the celebration, I realized with a pang that I would miss her as well. I felt a sudden rush of fear: What if she, too, were condemned to suffer my fate?

At sundown the guests took their leave and I dozed off, fully clothed, Haïfa at my side. My mother joined us a little later, after straightening up the room. When my father returned from his all-male meeting, we were fast asleep. During my last night in my parents' house, no dreams came to me, nor do I remember sleeping fitfully. I only wondered if I would awaken the next morning as if from a nightmare.

When sunlight flooded the room at around six o'clock the next morning, Omma woke me up and asked me to follow her out into the narrow hallway. As we did each morning, we bowed down before God, reciting the first prayer of the day. Then she served me a bowl of *ful* (fava beans cooked with onions and tomato sauce, which we eat at breakfast) and a cup of milky *chaï*, our tea. My little bundle was waiting for me in front of our door, but I pretended not to see it. It was only when a car horn sounded outside the house that I was forced to resign myself to this new life full of uncertainty. After hugging me

tightly, my mother helped me cover myself in a
black coat and scarf. For the past few years I had
worn simply a small colored veil when I went outside, and sometimes I even forgot it, but no one ever
paid any attention. Now I saw Omma reach into my
bundle and pull out a black *niqab*, which she handed
to me. Never, until that moment, had I been forced
to veil myself completely.

"From this day on, you must cover yourself when
going out into the street. You are now a married
woman. Your face must be seen by no one but your
husband. Because it is his *sharaf*, his honor, that is at
stake. And you must not disgrace it."

I nodded sadly and said good-bye to her. I was
angry at Omma for abandoning me, but could find
no words to tell her of my pain.

In the back of the SUV waiting in front of our door,
a short man was staring at me. He wore a long white
zanna, like Aba, and had a mustache. His short wavy
hair was somewhat mussed, his eyes brown, and his
face poorly shaved. His hands were stained with
black grease. He was not handsome. So this was Faez
Ali Thamer! The man who had asked for and been
granted my hand, that stranger whom I had perhaps
walked past one day in Khardji—where we had

returned for visits several times over the last few years—but whom I did not remember.

They had me sit in the middle row of seats, right behind the driver, with four other female passengers, including the wife of my husband's brother. Their smiles were strained, and they didn't seem very talkative. The stranger sat all the way in the back, next to his brother. I felt a little better not having to look at his face during our long ride, but I could feel his eyes on me, and it gave me the shivers. Who was he, actually? Why had he wanted to marry me? What was he expecting of me? And marriage—what exactly did that mean? I had no answers to those questions.

When the motor rumbled to life and the driver pulled away, my heart was pounding, and I couldn't help myself—I started crying, silently, with my face glued to the window as I watched Omma grow smaller and smaller until she was only a tiny little dot of nothing at all.

I never said a word that whole trip. Lost in my thoughts, I wanted only one thing: to find a way to go back home, to escape. The farther away from Sana'a the car drove on its way north, however, the more I understood how trapped I was. How many times did I wish I could tear off that stifling black *niqab?* I felt so small, too small for this whole business—for the *niqab*, for this long ride far away from my parents, for this new life beside a man who disgusted me, a man I didn't know. The vehicle stopped suddenly.

"Open the back door!"

The soldier's voice startled me. Exhausted from too much crying, I had finally fallen asleep. Then I remembered that the road north is full of checkpoints, and that we were only at the first one. People say it's because of the war raging in the north between the army and the Houthi rebels; my father says that the Houthis are Shiites, while most Yemenis are Sunnis. The difference? I have no idea. All I know is that I am Muslim and recite my five daily prayers.

After a glance inside the vehicle, the soldier sent us on our way. If only I could have taken that moment to appeal for his help, to ask him to save me! With his green uniform, his weapon on his shoulder, wasn't he supposed to ensure order and public safety? Then I could have told him that I didn't want to leave Sana'a, that I was afraid of being bored and alone out in that village, where I didn't know anyone anymore.

Over the years I'd grown used to Sana'a. I loved all the buildings under construction in the capital, the wide avenues, the billboard advertisements for cell phones and orange sodas that tickled the roof of my mouth. Pollution and traffic jams had become part of my daily life. But it was the old city, Bab al-Yemen—Yemen's Gate—that I would miss the most. Bab al-Yemen is truly a city within the city, a magical place where I loved to stroll around, holding Mona's or Jamila's hand, feeling as if I were an explorer off on a mission. It's a whole different universe, with its adobe houses and windows outlined in white tracery so delicate that Indian architects must clearly have passed through there long ago, well before my time. Bab al-Yemen is so elegantly civilized that I'd invented my own story of a king and queen from the olden days who must have lived out happy lives there. Perhaps the old city had even belonged entirely to them?

Anyone who enters Bab al-Yemen is immediately surrounded by all sorts of sounds: merchants' cries mingle with the popping and hissing of old cassette tapes and the laments of barefoot beggars, while a shoeshine boy at an intersection might grab your foot to offer you his services. The call to prayer often rises above this entire concert of jumbled noises. I used to have fun trying to sniff out the different smells of cumin, cinnamon, cloves, nuts, raisins—all the scents wafting from the street booths. Sometimes

I would stand on tiptoe to better appreciate the goods laid out in stalls that were a little too high for me, but whose bounty lay heaped up as far as the eye could see: silver *jambia*s, embroidered shawls, rugs, sugared doughnuts, henna, and dresses for little girls my age.

In Bab al-Yemen, we'd sometimes see women draped in *sitara*s ("curtains" in Arabic), large, colorful pieces of beautifully patterned cloth worn over their clothes. I used to call them "the ladies of the old city" because their brightly colored outfits were just so different from the black veils usually worn in the street that these women seemed to belong to another age.

One afternoon, when I was accompanying my aunt on some errands, I allowed myself to be distracted by this fantastic and almost unreal world, and I wandered off into the middle of the dense crowd. When I tried to retrace my steps to rejoin my aunt, I found that all the lanes and alleys looked alike. Should I take the next one on the right, or on the left? Disoriented, I crouched down in tears: I was well and truly lost. And it was only two hours later that I was spotted by a vendor who knew my aunt.

"Nujood, when will you stop being so scatter-brained?" Auntie had scolded me, grabbing my hand.

And here I was, lost again, on this sad day after

my wedding, sitting in the uncomfortable SUV, only now the people around me were grim and unfriendly. Gone were the magic of spices and the kindly looks of vendors who let children taste their still-warm doughnuts. My life was taking a new turn in this world of grown-ups, where dreams no longer had a place, faces became masks, and no one seemed to care about me.

Once the capital was behind us, the highway became a black ribbon snaking along among mountains and valleys. At every turn I clutched the armrest of my seat. My stomach was heaving, and several times I had to pinch myself, hard, to control my nausea. Better to die than to ask *him* to stop by the roadside so that I could breathe some fresh air, I thought. I kept gently swallowing my saliva as quietly as possible, trying not to be sick.

To block out everyone around me, I decided to observe the smallest details of the landscape. There were old fortresses in ruins perched on promontories; little brown houses with white trim that vaguely reminded me of Bab al-Yemen; cacti by the side of the road; arid mountain passes alternating with pockets of agriculture; goats cropping the grass; and cows. There were women, too, their faces partly hidden by the scarves they pulled over their mouths. I thought I also saw two run-over cats, but I closed my eyes quickly to avoid memorizing the image. When I opened them again, the car was driving through an ocean of khat. On the right, on the left, green as far as I could see. It was magnificent, so fresh and cool.

"Khat, our national tragedy!" exclaimed the driver. "It sucks up so much water that we'll all wind up dying of thirst in this country."

Life is really weird, I thought. *It's not just bad people who spread misery—even pretty things can be hurtful. So hard to understand . . .*

A little farther along, to my right, I recognized Cocabane, a small village cut into the living rock, way up atop a hill. I remembered going by the place with my parents when I was younger, on our way to another village to celebrate Eid. People say the women of Cocabane are thin and beautiful because they go every morning to labor in the fields. An hour to walk down, another to climb back up—a real workout. What courage! *An hour to walk down . . . another to climb back up. An hour to walk down . . .*

It was the throbbing of the car's engine that woke me with a start. How long had I been asleep? How many miles had we driven? I had no idea.

"One, two, three!"

Behind the vehicle, a half-dozen men were pushing on the bumper with all their strength, trying to free us from a sandy hole. Amid the dust cloud raised by the wheels, I tried to read the sign bearing the name of the dried-up village where we had run aground. Arjom. Apparently we had left the highway for a rocky, rutted road edging a ravine that led to a deep gorge. The car was definitely at a standstill.

"You'd do better to turn around," one of the villagers suggested. He had a red and white headcloth wrapped around his face. "You'll never get any farther; this track just keeps getting worse."

"But we must get to Khardji," insisted the driver.

"Pfft—with your car? You're joking."

"Well, then, how?"

"The best way is to go by donkey."

"Riding donkeys! But there are women with us. It might be difficult."

"Listen, why not hire one of our fellows? He's used to making round-trips carrying visitors. And the tires on his car are up to it—he gets new ones at least every two months, the road's so bad."

So we changed cars, and while the grown-ups were busy moving our bundles into the other one, I used those few minutes to stretch my legs. I took a deep breath, drawing as much pure mountain air into my lungs as possible. Below my black veil, the brown dress was sticking to my skin with perspiration, and I picked up the folds of material to go carefully over to the edge of the ravine. Right at the bottom, so far away, I recognized Wadi La'a, the valley of my village—it hadn't changed. I'd been so little, though, when we'd left. Were my childhood memories coming back, kept alive thanks to a few recent trips to the area with my parents? Or was I recalling things from the faded photographs languishing in an old album that Aba looked at from time to time with tears in his eyes? I saw my grandfather again in my mind's eye, my Jad, whom I had loved so much. It had been a year since his death, when I had cried and cried. He always wore a white turban, and although his beard was thin and grizzled, he had bushy, dark brown eyebrows. Sometimes he would sit me on his knees and playfully tip me over backward, then catch me at the last minute. I'd grown used to the idea that if the world collapsed around me, my Jad would always be there to save me. He had gone too soon.

"Nujood! Nujood!"

I turned around, wondering who could be calling me in that unfamiliar voice, so strange to my ears.

Not like Jad's, a voice I could always recognize with my eyes closed. Looking up, I realized that it was *him*, my unknown husband, speaking to me for the first time since we'd left Sana'a. With barely a glance at me, he announced that it was time to leave again. Nodding, I headed toward our new "carriage": a rusted-out red and white Toyota pickup. I was put in the front seat with the veiled sister-in-law, sitting on the new driver's right. The men clambered into the open truck bed in the back, with other passengers who were catching a ride.

"Hang on tight," warned the driver. "The pickup will rock back and forth."

Before setting out, he turned on his tape deck at top volume, and folk music began crackling out of loudspeakers as rusty as the pickup. The vibrations of the oud, a kind of Oriental lute, accompanied the voice of a very well-known local singer, Hussein Moheb, and soon they were joined by the jolting of the pickup doing battle with the big stones in the road. We weren't rocking back and forth, though; we were flying in all directions! Several times, stones crashed into our windshield, and I hung on for dear life, praying to arrive at the village in one piece.

"Listen to the music, it will make you forget your fear!" shouted the driver.

If he had only known what other fears tormented me.

Hour after hour we drove, to the sound of Hussein Moheb's wailing; I should have counted the number of times the driver rewound the cassette. He seemed intoxicated by the music, which surely gave him the courage to forge ahead. Hanging on to his steering wheel like a rider clinging to his horse, he tackled even the slightest turn with his eyes riveted on the winding road, as if he knew all its pitfalls by heart.

"God made nature tough, but luckily he made men even tougher!"

Well, I thought, *if the driver is right, then God must have forgotten to include me.*

The deeper into the valley we went, the worse I felt. I was tired. I felt sick to my stomach. I was hungry and thirsty. But most of all, I was afraid. The closer we came to Wadi La'a, the more uncertain my fate seemed. And my hopes for escape? Dashed.

Khardji hadn't changed; it still felt like the end of the earth. As soon as we arrived, aching from the bone-jarring ride, I recognized the five stone houses, the modest river flowing through the village, the bees humming from flower to flower, the endless trees, and the village children going to the well to fill their little yellow jerry cans. A woman was waiting for us on the threshold of one of the houses. I felt immediately that she didn't like me. She didn't embrace me—not even a tiny kiss, not even a gentle pat. *His* mother. My new mother-in-law. She was old and ugly, with skin as wrinkled as a lizard's. She was missing two of her front teeth, while the others were rotten from cavities and blackened by tobacco. She wore a black and gray head scarf. She gestured for me to enter. The inside of the house was spare, with hardly any furnishings: four bedrooms, a living room, a tiny kitchen. The toilet was out under the stars, behind some bushes.

I hadn't eaten anything since we'd left Sana'a; I was famished and fairly fell upon the rice and meat that *his* sisters had prepared. Joined after our meal by some guests from the village, the grown-ups gathered to chew khat. Again! Huddled in a corner, I watched them in silence. To my astonishment, no one seemed surprised by my tender age. Later I learned that marriages to little girls are not unusual in the countryside, so for these people, I didn't seem like an exception. There is even a tribal proverb that says, "To guarantee a happy marriage, marry a nine-year-old girl."

The grown-ups were chatting up a storm.

"Life in Sana'a has become so expensive," my sister-in-law was complaining.

"As of tomorrow, I'm going to teach the child to work like the rest of us," announced my mother-in-law, without saying my name. "And I certainly hope she brought some money with her."

"No more time for girlish fancies. We'll show her how to be a woman, a real one."

I remember how relieved I felt when they led me to my room, after the guests had gone at sunset. That brown tunic I'd been wearing since the day before was starting to smell really foul, and now I could finally take it off. Once the door had shut behind me, I sighed deeply and quickly slipped into a little red cotton shirt I'd brought from Sana'a. It smelled like home, a musty smell with a hint of resinous incense, a familiar and comforting scent. A long woven mat was lying on the floor: my bed. Beside it was an old oil lamp that cast the shadow of its flame on the wall. I didn't even need to put out the light to fall asleep.

I would rather have never awakened. When the door crashed open, I was startled awake, and thought that the night wind must have come up unusually strong. I'd barely opened my eyes when I felt a damp, hairy body pressing against me. Someone had blown out the lamp, leaving the room pitch dark. I shivered. It was *him*! I recognized him right away from that over-powering odor of cigarettes and khat. He stank! Like an animal! Without a word, he began to rub himself against me.

"Please, I'm begging you, leave me alone," I gasped. I was shaking.

"You are my wife! From now on, I decide every-thing. We must sleep in the same bed."

I leapt to my feet, ready to run away. Where? What did it matter—I had to escape from this trap. Then he stood up, too. The door was not com-pletely closed, and spying a glimmer of light from the moon and stars, I dashed immediately toward the courtyard.

He ran after me.

"Help! Help!" I shrieked, sobbing.

My voice rang in the night, but it was as if I were shouting into a void. I ran everywhere, anywhere, panting for breath. I went into one room but ducked out again when he followed me there. I ran without looking back. I stumbled over something, maybe a piece of glass, and scrambled to my feet to take off again, but arms caught me, held me tightly, wrestled me back into the bedroom, pushed me down on the mat. I felt paralyzed, as if I had been tied down.

Hoping to find a female ally, I called out to my mother-in-law.

"*Amma!* Auntie!"

There was no reply. I screamed again.

"Somebody help me!"

When he took off his white tunic, I rolled into a ball to protect myself, but he began pulling at my nightshirt, wanting me to undress. Then he ran his rough hands over my body and pressed his lips against mine. He smelled so awful, a mixture of tobacco and onion.

I tried to get away again, moaning, "Get away from me! I'll tell my father!"

"You can tell your father whatever you like. He signed the marriage contract. He gave me permission to marry you."

"You have no right!"

"Nujood, you are my wife!"

"Help! Help!"

He started to laugh, nastily.

"I repeat: you are my wife. Now you must do what I want! Got that?"

Suddenly it was as if I'd been snatched up by a hurricane, flung around, struck by lightning, and I had no more strength to fight back. There was a peal of thunder, and another, and another—the sky was falling down on me, and it was then that something burning, a burning I had never felt before, invaded the deepest part of me. No matter how I screamed, no one came to help me. It hurt, awfully, and I was all alone to face the pain.

With what felt like my last breath, I shrieked one more time, I think, and then lost consciousness.

5

Shada

April 9, 2008

With her cell phone glued to her ear, Shada is pacing up and down the courthouse hall.

"We need to do everything we can to get Nujood out of the clutches of her husband. We must alert the press, the women's groups. . . ."

After she finishes her call, she leans down to me, crouching to put herself at my height.

"Don't be afraid, Nujood. I'll help you get your divorce."

No one has ever shown so much concern for me before.

Shada is a lawyer. People say she's a very important lawyer, one of the best lady lawyers in Yemen, who fights for women's rights. I look at her, my eyes wide with admiration. She's beautiful, and so sweet. Her voice is a little shrill, and if she talks quickly, it's only because she's in a great hurry. She smells of nice perfume, with the scent of jasmine. As soon as I saw her, I liked her. Unlike the women in my family, she doesn't cover her face, and that's rare in Yemen, not wearing the *niqab*. Shada wears a long, black, silky coat, with just a colored scarf on her head. Her skin glows, and her lipstick makes her look chic, like ladies in films. And when she wears her sunglasses, she looks like a movie star. What a contrast to all those veiled women out in the streets!

"With me, you've nothing to fear," she says, patting my face reassuringly.

Shada approached me this morning as soon as she spotted me. When everyone returned to work at the courthouse after the weekend, she heard all about me, and was very upset by my story. She decided that she absolutely had to meet me. I was in the courtyard when she called out to me.

"Excuse me, are you the little girl who came looking for a divorce?"

"Yes, that's me."

"Heavens! Follow me; we simply have to talk," she said.

So much has happened these last few days that my head is still in a whirl. During the entire weekend—

Thursday and Friday, in Yemen—Judge Abdel Wahed and his wife were especially good to me. I was treated to toys, tasty food, hot showers, and good-night kisses, like a real child. Inside the house, I even had permission to take off my married woman's veil, the one my mother-in-law makes me adjust as soon as it starts to slip. What happiness, not to fear blows from a stick, or tremble at the thought of going to bed, or flinch at the slightest sound of a door closing. Yet in spite of all this kind attention, my nights are still very uneasy, because as soon as I fall asleep, I feel as though the storm were lying in wait for me, and if I close my eyes for too long, the door might fly open again, and the monster return. What terror, what suffering! Judge Abdel Wahed says that this is normal, that I'll need time to forget all my pain.

When he brought me back to the courthouse on Saturday morning, it was hard to return to reality. At nine o'clock we were already sitting in his office, along with the other two judges, Abdo and Mohammad al-Ghazi, who smiled kindly at me when I came in. But here's the thing: Mohammad al-Ghazi was very worried.

"According to Yemeni law, it is difficult for you to file a complaint against your husband and your father," he told me.

"Why is that?"

"It's a little complicated for a child your age, and hard to explain," he answered. Then he talked about several obstacles. Like many children born in Yemeni villages, I didn't have any identification documents—not even a birth certificate. And I was too young to initiate proceedings against anyone. Such reasons were easy for a learned man like Mohammad al-Ghazi to understand, but not me. Still, I felt, I ought to keep a positive outlook; at least I had found some nice judges who wanted to help me. After all, they were not obliged to take up my case and could have ignored my plight, as many others had, and advised me to go home to fulfill my duties as a wife. A contract had been signed, and unanimously approved by the men of my family. According to Yemeni tradition, it was therefore valid.

"For the moment," Mohammad al-Ghazi told his colleagues, "we must act quickly. So I suggest that we place Nujood's father and husband under temporary arrest. If we want to protect her, it's better to have them in prison than at liberty."

Prison! That's very serious punishment. Would Aba ever forgive me? I was suddenly consumed with shame and guilt. And I felt dreadful when they asked me to go with the soldier who would arrest them, to make sure he found the right address. My family hadn't seen me all weekend and must certainly have thought that, like my brother Fares, I had run away forever. I didn't even want to imagine what my mother must have wondered when my brothers and sisters started clamoring for the bread I'd been sent to buy for breakfast. Besides, I was thinking about how my father had recently fallen ill, and had even begun coughing up blood. Could he survive imprisonment? If he were to die, I'd never forgive myself.

But I had no choice. Abdo had explained to me that when people are suffering, the evildoers must be punished. So I got into the car with the soldier. When we arrived at my parents' house, however, the door was locked. I felt strangely relieved, and a few hours later, when the soldier went back there, he no longer needed me to show him the way.

That very evening, the judges decided to find a safe place for me to stay. In Yemen there are no shelters for girls like me, but I couldn't very well remain forever with Abdel Wahed and his family, who had already done so much for me.

"Who is your favorite uncle?" one of the judges asked.

My favorite uncle? I thought the best choice would be Shoyi, Omma's brother, a former soldier in the Yemeni army, now retired: a big, strong man with a certain prestige in my family. He lived in Beit Boss, a neighborhood far from ours, with his two wives and seven children. True, he hadn't opposed my marriage, but he represented the forces of order, in a way—and he, at least, did not beat his daughters.

Shoyi was not very talkative, which suited me fine. He didn't ask me too many questions, and he let me play with my cousins. That evening, before falling asleep, I thanked God for not allowing Shoyi to reproach me for my boldness, or even mention my running away. Basically, I think my uncle was as discomfited as I was by the whole thing.

The next three days seemed long to me, full of the same tedious things. I spent most of my time at the courthouse, hoping for a miracle, some unforeseen solution. Unfortunately, the future wasn't clear. The judges had promised to do their utmost to grant me a divorce, but they needed time. It's funny, but going every day to that big, bustling courtyard, I finally became used to the tremendous crowd that had so impressed me at first. I could recognize the young tea and juice vendors even at a distance. The boy with the scale was always busy weighing visitors who had time to kill, and now I sometimes smiled encouragingly at him. As for me, though, whenever I returned to the courtyard I felt a pang of discouragement. How many times would I have to go there before I could again become just an ordinary little girl? Abdo had warned me that my case was most unusual. But what do judges do when faced with one like that? I had no idea.

But I believe I am learning the answer from Shada, the beautiful lawyer with sunglasses. When she came up to me for the first time, I saw how she looked at me with great emotion before exclaiming "Heavens!" Then she checked her watch, opened her appointment book, and completely rearranged her heavy schedule. She began calling her family, friends, and colleagues; several times I heard her say, "I have to take on an important case, a very important case."

This woman seems to have endless determination. Abdel Wahed is right: she's an impressive lawyer. She must have lots of power; her cell phone never stops ringing, and everyone she encounters always greets her very politely.

"Nujood, you're like a daughter to me. I won't abandon you," she whispers to me.

I'm beginning to believe it. She has no reason to lie to me. I feel at ease with Shada, and I feel safe with her. She knows how to find exactly the right words, and her lilting voice comforts me. If the world came tumbling down, I know that she would stand by me. With her, I feel for the first time the maternal tenderness my mother, too preoccupied by all her family worries, did not know how—or rather, had no time—to give me.

But there's still one nagging question.

"Shada?" I ask timidly.

"Yes, Nujood?"

"May I ask you something?"

"Of course."

"Can you promise me that I will never return to my husband's house?"

"*Insha'Allah*, Nujood. I'll do my very best to keep him from hurting you again. All will be well. All will be well. But . . ."

"But what?"

"You must be strong, because it may take some time."

"How much time?"

"Don't think about that right now. Tell yourself that the hardest part is over. The hardest part was having the strength to escape, and you carried that off beautifully."

When I sigh, Shada gives me a little smile and pats me on the head. She's so tall and slender. She impresses me a lot.

"And now, may I ask you a question?" she says.

"Yes."

"How did you find the courage to run away—all the way to the courthouse?"

"The courage to run away? I couldn't bear *his* meanness anymore. I couldn't."

6

Running Away

In Khardji, life had become impossible. Tortured by shame and pain, I suffered in silence. All those horrible things *he* made me endure, day after day, night after night—whom could I tell about them? In fact, that first evening, I realized that nothing would ever be the same again.

"*Mabrouk!* Congratulations!"

Early-morning light pours into the bedroom. In the distance, a rooster is crowing. Staring down at my naked little body, my mother-in-law taps my cheek to wake me. I can remember her face as if it were yesterday. Behind the old woman's shoulder I recognize my sister-in-law, the one who rode in the car with us. I'm still drenched in perspiration. Eyes wide, I look around at the disorder of the bedroom: the oil lamp has rolled over to the door, and the brown dress lies in a heap on the floor like an old dishrag. And there *he* is, on the mat, sound asleep. What a *wahesh*—what a monster! On the rumpled sheet, I see a little streak of blood.

"Congratulations!" echoes my sister-in-law.

With a sly smile, she studies the red stain. I can't say a word. I feel paralyzed. Then my mother-in-law bends down to pick me up as if I were a package. Why didn't she come earlier, when I needed her help? Now, in any case, it's too late—unless she was his accomplice in what he just did to me? Jabbing her hands into my ribs, she pushes the door aside with her foot and carries me to the narrow little bathroom, where I see a tub and a bucket. She begins splashing water on me, and oh, it's cold!

"*Mabrouk!*" both women say together.

Their voices buzz in my tired ears, and I feel small, so small. I've lost control of my body, my movements. I'm cold on the outside, but inside, I'm burning. It's as if there were something dirty in me. I'm angry, but can't manage to put my anger into words. *Omma, you're too far away for me to call to you for help. Aba, why did you marry me off? Why, why me? And why didn't anyone warn me about what was going to happen to me? Whatever did I do to deserve this?*

I want to go home!

A few hours later, when *he* finally wakes up, I turn my head away to avoid looking into his eyes. He heaves a great sigh, eats his breakfast, and disappears for the day. Huddled in a corner, I pray for God the Almighty to come save me. I hurt everywhere. I'm terrified at the idea of spending my whole life with this beast. I've fallen into a trap, and I can't get out.

I had to adjust quickly to a new life: I had no right to leave the house, no right to fetch water from the stream, no right to complain, no right to say no. And school? Out of the question, even though I was dying to write my name in white chalk on a big blackboard and sit on a bench to hear the teacher tell us new stories.

Khardji, my native village, had become foreign to me. At the house, during the day, I had to obey my mother-in-law's orders: cut up the vegetables, feed the chickens, prepare tea for any guests who dropped by, wash the floor, do the dishes. No matter how hard I scrubbed the grease-blackened pots, they would never return to their original color. The towels were gray and smelled bad. Flies buzzed around me. Whenever I stopped for a moment, my mother-in-law pulled my hair with her filthy hands. I wound up as sticky as the kitchen, and my fingernails were completely black.

One morning I asked her permission to go play with the children my age.

"You're not on holiday here," she grumbled.

"Please, just for a few minutes?"

"Impossible! A married woman cannot allow herself to be seen with just anyone—that's all we need, for you to go ruining our reputation. We're not in the capital here! In Khardji, people notice everything, hear everything, know everything. So you'd better be careful, and don't you dare forget what I've told you, understand? Or I'll tell your husband."

He left every morning and returned right before sunset. When he got home, he had his meal served to him on the *sofrah* and never helped clear the table. Each time I heard *him* arrive, the same panic seized my heart.

When night fell, I knew what would begin again. Again and again. The same savagery, the same pain and distress. The door slamming, the oil lamp rolling across the floor, and the sheets getting all twisted up. "*Ya, beint!* Hey, girl!" That's what he would yell before throwing himself on me.

He never said my first name.

It was on the third day that *he* began hitting me. *He* could not bear my attempts to resist him. When I would try to keep him from lying down on the mat next to me after he'd extinguished the lamp, *he* would start to hit me, first with his hands, then with a stick. Thunder and lightning, over and over. And his mother egged him on.

Whenever *he* would complain about me, she would tell him hoarsely, "Hit her even harder. She must listen to you—she's your wife."

"*Ya, beint!*" he'd yell, and run after me again.

"You have no right!" I sobbed.

"I'm tired of your whining—I didn't marry you to listen to you snivel all the time," he would shout, baring his big yellow teeth.

It hurt me to be talked to that way, with such contempt, and he made fun of me in front of others. I lived in permanent fear of more slaps and blows. Occasionally he even used his fists. Every day, fresh bruises on my back, new wounds on my arms. And that burning in my belly. I felt dirty everywhere. When women neighbors visited my mother-in-law, I heard them whispering among themselves, and sometimes they would point at me. What were they saying?

Whenever I could, I would go hide in a corner, lost and bewildered. My teeth chattered when I thought of the coming night. I was alone, so alone. No one to confide in, no one to talk to. I hated *him*— I loathed them all. They were disgusting! Did every married girl have to go through the same agony? Or was I the only one to suffer like this? I felt no love whatsoever for this stranger. Had my parents felt any for each other? With *him,* I finally understood the real meaning of the word *cruelty*.

Days and nights went by like this. Ten, twenty, thirty? I no longer remember precisely. In the evening, I was taking longer and longer to fall asleep. Each time *he* came to do his vile things to me at night, I lay awake afterward. During the day, I dozed, abandoned, distraught—I was losing all sense of time. I missed Sana'a, and school. My brothers and sisters, too: Abdo's constant liveliness, Morad's clowning, Mona's jokes (on her good days), little Rawdha's nursery rhymes. More and more, I thought of Haïfa, hoping she wouldn't be married off like me. As the days passed, I began to forget the details of their faces: the color of their skin, the shape of their noses, the folds of their dimples. I needed to see them again.

Every morning I wept, begging my in-laws to send me to my parents. I had no way to contact Aba and Omma; there was no electricity in Khardji, so a telephone? Forget it. No planes passed over my village, no buses came, no cars. I could have sent my family a letter, but I didn't know how to write much more than my first name and a few simple words. Still, I had to find some way back to Sana'a.

Escape? I thought about it a few times. But where to? Since I knew no one in the village, it would have been hard for me to seek refuge with a neighbor or beg a traveler on a donkey to save me. Khardji, my native village, had become my prison.

Then one morning, worn down by all my crying, *he* told me *he* would allow me to visit my parents. At last! He would go with me and stay with his brother in Sana'a, but afterward, he insisted, we had to return to the village. I rushed to gather my things before *he* changed his mind.

The trip home seemed quicker than our previous journey, but the same hideous images still disturbed my sleep whenever I nodded off: the bloodstained sheet, my mother-in-law's face looming over me, the bucket of icy water. And suddenly, I would start awake. No! I would never go back, never. Khardji, the end of the earth: I never wanted to set foot there again.

"It is out of the question for you to leave your husband!"

I had not expected my father's unyielding reaction, which quickly put an end to the joy of my return to Sana'a. As for my mother, she kept quiet, simply raising her arms to heaven and murmuring,

"That's how life is, Nujood: all women must endure this; we have all gone through the same thing."

But why hadn't she said anything to me? Why hadn't she warned me? Now that the marriage vows had been said, I was trapped, unable to retreat. No matter what I told my parents about my nightly suffering—the beatings, the burning, and all those dreadful personal things I was ashamed to speak of—they still insisted that it was my duty to live with him.

"I don't love him! He isn't nice to me. He hurts me. He forces me to do nasty things that make me sick."

"Nujood," repeated my father, "you are a married woman now. You must stay with your husband."

"No, I don't want to! I want to come home!"

"Impossible."

"Please, please!"

"It's a matter of *sharaf*, you hear me?"

"But—"

"Listen to me!"

"Aba, I—"

"If you divorce your husband, my brothers and cousins will kill me! *Sharaf*, honor, comes first. Honor! Do you understand?"

No, I didn't understand, and I couldn't understand. Not only was *he* hurting me, but my family, my own family, was defending him. All that for a question of—what was it? Honor. But this word everyone kept using, exactly what did it mean? I was dumbfounded.

Haïfa watched with big eyes, understanding still less than I did about what was happening to me. Seeing me burst into tears, she slipped her hand into mine, her way of telling me she was on my side. And once more, horrified, I wondered: What if they were planning on marrying her off, too? Haïfa, my little sister, my pretty little sister . . . Let her at least have a chance to escape this nightmare.

Mona tried several times to defend me, but she was too timid, and anyway, who would have listened to her? Here it's always the oldest, and the men, who have the last word. Poor Mona! I realized that if I wanted to break free, I could count on no one but myself.

And I was running out of time. I had to find a solution before *he* came back to get me. I had managed to wangle his permission to stay with my parents for a while, but I was going around in circles, with no escape in sight. "Nujood must remain by her husband's side," my father kept saying. Whenever he wasn't there, I hurried to talk to my mother, who cried and told me she missed me, but could do nothing for me.

I was right to be afraid. *He* soon came visiting, to

remind me of my duties as a wife. I tried to refuse, but it was no use. After some argument, *he* agreed to let me remain a few more weeks in Sana'a, but only if I stayed with him at his brother's house. He didn't trust me, suspecting that I would run away if I stayed too long with my parents. So for more than a month, I was plunged back into hell.

"When will you stop all your moaning? I'm fed up with it," he complained one day, glaring and shaking his fist at me.

"When you let me go back to my parents' house!" I buried my face in my hands.

Thanks to my stubbornness, I finally won a new reprieve.

"But this is the last time," he warned me.

Back home, I realized I would have to act quickly if I wanted to get rid of that man and avoid being dragged back to Khardji. Five days passed, five difficult days during which I kept running into walls. My father, my brothers, my uncles—no one would listen to me.

Knocking on every possible door in search of someone who would, I went to see Dowla, my father's second wife, who lived with her five children in a tiny first-floor apartment in an old building at the end of a blind alley, right across from our street.

Driven by my anguish at the thought of returning to Khardji, I climbed the stairs, holding my nose to avoid the stench of garbage and communal toilets. Dowla opened her door wearing a long red and black dress and a huge smile.

"*Ya*, Nujood! What a surprise to see you again. Welcome!"

I liked Dowla. She had olive skin and long hair, which she kept braided. Tall, slender, she was prettier than Omma, and always endlessly patient—she never scolded me. The poor woman hadn't had an easy time of it, though. Married late, at twenty, and to my father, who neglected her completely, she had learned to rely solely on herself. Her oldest boy, Yahya, eight, was born handicapped; still unable to walk, he required special attention, and his tantrums could last several hours. In spite of her poverty, which forced her to beg in the street to pay her paltry rent and buy bread for her children, Dowla was incredibly generous.

She invited me to sit on the big straw pallet that took up half the room, next to the tiny stove where water was boiling. She often had to fill her little ones' bottles with tea instead of milk. Hanging from hooks on the wall, the plastic bags she used as her "pantry" looked far from full.

"Nujood," she ventured, "you seem very worried."

I knew that she was one of the few members of my

family who had opposed my marriage, but no one had bothered to listen to her. She, on whom life had not smiled, had always shown compassion for those even less well off than she was. I felt I could trust her, and knew I need hide nothing from her.

"I've so much to tell you," I replied, and then I poured out my heart.

Frowning, she listened to my story, which seemed to affect her deeply. She thought quietly for a moment, busying herself at the stove, then poured me some boiling tea in the only glass Yahya had not yet broken. Handing it to me, she leaned over and looked into my eyes.

"Nujood," she whispered, "if no one will listen to you, you must just go straight to court."

"To what?"

"To court!"

To court—but of course! In a flash, I saw images of judges in turbans, lawyers always in a hurry, men in white *zanna*s and veiled women coming to complain about complicated family problems, thefts, squabbles over inheritances. Now I remembered what a court-room was: I'd seen one on television, in a show Haïfa and I used to watch at the neighbors' house. The actors spoke an Arabic different from ours here in Yemen, with a strange accent, and I thought I remembered that the program was from Kuwait. In the large room where the plaintiffs appeared one after another, the walls were white, and several rows of brown wooden benches faced the judge. We'd see the defendants arrive in a van with bars on the windows.

"Go to the courthouse," Dowla continued. "As far as I know, that's the only place where you'll get a hearing. Ask to see the judge—after all, he's the government's representative. He's very powerful, a godfather to all of us. His job is to help victims."

Dowla had convinced me. From that moment on, my thoughts became much clearer. If my parents wouldn't help me, well, I'd act all on my own. My mind was made up: I'd do whatever I had to. I was ready to climb mountains to keep from finding myself lying on that mat again, night after night, all alone against that monster. I hugged Dowla tightly in thanks.

"Nujood?"

"Yes?"

"Take this, it might help."

She slipped two hundred rials into my hand, the entire pittance—worth barely a dollar—she'd managed to beg that very morning at a neighboring intersection.

"Thank you, Dowla. Thank you!"

The next morning I woke up with more energy than usual, and even surprised myself with my new attitude. As I did every morning, I washed my face, said my prayer, and lit the tiny stove to boil water for tea. Then, fiddling nervously with my hands, I waited impatiently for my mother to get up. *Nujood*, said my little inner voice, *try to behave as naturally as possible, so you don't arouse suspicion.*

When Omma finally arose a little later and began undoing the corner of the black scarf where she usually hides her coins, I understood with relief that my plan might just work.

"Nujood," she said, handing over 150 rials, "Off you go; buy some bread for breakfast."

"Yes, Omma," I replied obediently.

I took the money. I put on my coat and my black scarf, the clothes of a married woman. I carefully closed the door behind me. The nearby lanes and alleys were still half empty; I took the first street on the right, the one leading to the corner bakery, where the bread is deliciously crusty when it has just come out of the old-fashioned oven. As I walked along I heard the familiar song of the vendor who sells gas bottles every day from a little cart he pulls along behind his bicycle.

I was drawing closer and closer to the bakery, and could already inhale the wonderful smell of the *khobz* loaves, piping hot. Soon I saw that several local women were already in line in front of the tandoor. At the last minute, however, I changed direction, heading for the main avenue of our neighborhood. "The courthouse," Dowla had told me, "all you have to do is go to the courthouse."

Once on the avenue, I was suddenly afraid of being recognized. What if one of my uncles passed by? I felt shaky inside; hoping to hide, I brought the folds of my scarf over almost my entire face, leaving only my eyes uncovered. For once, this *niqab* I'd never wanted to wear again after leaving Khardji turned out to be quite useful. I avoided looking back, for fear of being followed. In front of me, buses were waiting, lined up along the sidewalk. In front of a grocery store selling plastic balloons, I recognized the yellow and white six-seat minibus that passes through the neighborhood every day, taking passengers to the center of town, not far from Al-Tahrir Square. *Go on. If you want a divorce, it's up to you,* said my little voice encouragingly. I waited in line like everyone else. The other children my age were with their parents; I was the only girl waiting on her own. I looked down at the ground, to discourage any questions. I had the awful sensation that my plan was written on my forehead.

The driver got down from his seat to open the

door, sliding it over to one side. The pushing began immediately, with several women elbowing one another to get inside. I jumped right in, hoping only to get out of my neighborhood as quickly as possible, before my parents realized I was missing and alerted the police. I took a seat in the back between an elderly lady and a younger woman, both veiled from head to toe. Sandwiched between their corpulent bodies, I was shielded from sight if anyone glanced in from the street. Luckily, neither of the women asked me any questions.

When the engine started up, I felt my heart beat wildly; I remembered my brother Fares, and the courage he'd shown in fleeing our house four years earlier. He had succeeded, so why shouldn't I? But did I even truly understand what I was doing? What would my father have said if he'd seen his daughter get on a public bus all by herself? In so doing, was I staining his honor, as he put it?

The door closed, and it was too late to change my mind. Through the window I watched the city stream by: cars trapped in the morning traffic jams; buildings under construction; black-veiled women; peddlers hawking jasmine flowers, chewing gum, and tissues. Sana'a was so big, so full of people! Between the dusty labyrinth of the capital and the isolation of Khardji, I liked Sana'a a thousand times more.

"End of the line!" shouted the driver.

We'd arrived, and the door had hardly begun to slide open when the hubbub of the stret invaded the minibus. I joined the press of women passengers hurrying to get off, and with trembling fingers handed a few coins to the conductor to pay for my ride. I had no idea at all where the courthouse was, however, and didn't dare ask my fellow passengers for directions. I was overwhelmed with anxiety, as well as the simple fear of getting lost. I looked right, left; a policeman at a broken red light was attempting to keep some order among the madly rushing cars, their horns blaring, trying to pass one another on all sides. I blinked, half dazzled by the rays of the morning sun in the bright blue sky. How could I ever cross a street in such chaos? I would never make it alive. Huddled by a streetlight, I was trying to collect my thoughts when I caught sight of a yellow vehicle. I was saved.

It was one of the many taxis that crisscross the city at all hours of the day and night. In Yemen, as soon as a boy can reach the accelerator, his father buys him a driving license in the hope that he'll land a job as a driver, to help feed the family. I'd already taken such taxis, going to Bab al-Yemen with Mona.

Thinking he would surely have every address in Sana'a at his fingertips, I raised my hand and

signaled him to stop. A young girl, alone, in a taxi—
that's simply not done. But by this time, I couldn't
have cared less about what people might think.

"I want to go to the courthouse!" I exclaimed to
the driver, who stared at me in astonishment.

I sat quietly in the back for the entire ride. His
cheek bulging with khat, the driver had no idea how
grateful I was to him for not challenging me with
questions. He was, without knowing it, the silent accomplice of my flight. With my right arm pressed
over my stomach, I tried discreetly to control my
rapid breathing, and closed my eyes.

"Here we are!"

With a sharp stab on the brake, he pulled his car
up by the courtyard gate in front of an imposing
building. The courthouse! A traffic policeman impatiently waved him on because he was blocking the
way. I hurried out of the taxi and handed him the rest
of my money. After that exploit, I suddenly felt
wildly daring. Confused and terrified, true, but full
of spirit! God willing, my life was going to change
completely.

7

The Divorce

April 15, 2008

The great day has arrived sooner than expected. What a crush! The courtroom is full to bursting; it's amazing. Have all these people on the benches in front of the judge's raised desk come just for me? Although Shada warned me that the preliminaries might take a great deal of time, her media campaign has paid off, and now, in this jam-packed courtroom, she seems as astonished as I am. One week has passed since our first meeting: a week spent contacting newspapers, TV networks, and feminist organizations. And this is the result: a miracle. I have never seen so many snapshot and film cameras in my life. I'm breathing faster and faster—are all these faces crowding in around me using up my oxygen, or am I simply a bundle of nerves? Beneath my black scarf, I'm perspiring heavily.

"Nujood, a smile!" shouts a photographer, elbowing his way over to me.

Almost immediately, a row of cameras forms in front of me. I blush, intimidated by all these flashbulbs. Besides, I can't see anyone I know in this throng of faces, all looking at me. I cling to Shada. Her scent reassures me, the smell of jasmine I now know so well.

"Khaleh Shada? Auntie?"

"Yes, Nujood?"

"I'm scared."

"It's going to work out. It will be all right," she whispers to me.

I would never have imagined stirring up so much interest. Me! A silent victim for so many months, suddenly propelled into the spotlight, facing all these journalists. Shada had promised me that they wouldn't come, that it would just be us. Whatever can I say to them if they start asking me questions? No one ever taught me how to answer questions.

"Shada?"

"Yes, Nujood?"

"All these flashes—I feel like . . . George Bush, the important American who's on television so much."

"Don't worry about it," she says, and smiles.

I pretend to smile back. But deep down I feel frozen solid, unable to move, with the strange feeling that my feet are nailed to the ground. I do understand, however, that if I am frightened, it's because I really don't know what I'm up against: Just how does a divorce happen? I forgot to ask Shada. I never heard anything about it in school. My best friend, Malak, and I always told each other everything, but we never talked about this. Maybe we thought it was just for adults, and we were obviously too little to bother with grown-up stuff. I don't even know whether my teachers were married or divorced—I never thought to ask them. So I can't very well compare my situation to that of any of the women I know.

And then, like a blinding flash that brings on a headache, a chilling thought occurs to me: What if the monster simply says no? What can I say, in fact, if he decides to oppose our separation, if he begins threatening the judge with his *jambia*, backed up by his brothers and the men of the village?

"Don't worry, it's going to go well," Shada reassures me, patting my shoulder.

I look up at her. I don't believe she slept much last night; she has little bags under her eyes. She seems exhausted. I feel bad, because it's my fault, all of this. And yet, even though she's tired, she's still beautiful and elegant—a real city lady. I notice that she's wearing a different scarf, a pink one, to match her tunic. One of my favorite colors! And she's in a long gray skirt with high heels. I'm so lucky she's right beside me. Shada, my second mother.

Suddenly I see a hand waving at me from the crowd. Finally, someone I recognize. It's Hamed Thabet, a reporter for the *Yemen Times*, my new friend. A real big brother, not like Mohammad. Someone Shada knows introduced him to us. He's tall, with brown hair, a round face, broad shoulders, and his kindness touched me immediately. I don't know exactly how old he is; I didn't dare ask him. We met a few days ago, in the courthouse yard, almost in the same spot where Shada found me that first time.

He asked me if he could take my picture, and then we went to a small restaurant near the courthouse, where he pulled out his pen and notebook to ply me with questions about my parents, my marriage, Khardji, my wedding night. I flushed with shame telling him my story, but when I saw him wince as I described the bloodstain on the sheet, I understood that he sympathized with me. I even saw him quietly tapping his pen on the table, as if he were trying to hide his feelings, but I couldn't help noticing his distress. He was angry, felt terrible for me, and it showed.

"But you're so little! How could he do that?" he murmured.

Strangely enough, I didn't cry this time, and after a few minutes of silence, I continued.

"I wanted to play outside, like all children my age, but he beat me and kept making me go back into the bedroom with him to do the nasty things he wanted. He always used bad words with me. . . ."

By the time we said good-bye, Hamed's notebook pages were black with writing. He had written down even the slightest details. Then he managed to sneak into the prison to take pictures of Aba and the monster with his cell phone. A few days later, Shada told me that Hamed's article had been published and had caused a huge stir in Yemen. He was the first journalist to break my story to the public. I was upset at the time, it's true, but now I know that I owe him a great deal.

At the entrance to the courtroom, the cameras begin to jostle for a good view.

I shiver: I recognize Aba and . . . the monster, escorted by two soldiers in olive-green uniforms and black kepis. The prisoners look furious. Passing in front of us, the monster lowers his eyes, then abruptly turns back to Shada.

"Proud of yourself, hey? I didn't have a real celebration for my marriage, but you're certainly throwing a party for us here," he snarls.

How dare he speak to her like that? Just what I dreaded is now happening, but Shada remains marvelously calm. She doesn't even blink. This woman has a strength of character that astounds me. She doesn't need to wave her arms all around to express her feelings; the look in her eyes reveals all the contempt she feels for *him*. That look is enough. I've learned a lot from her, these past few days.

"Don't listen to him," she tells me.

Try as I might to control my emotions the way Shada does, I can't. Not yet, at least. My heart pounds; I can't help it. After all that *he* has done to me, I hate *him* so much! When I look up, I find myself staring into Aba's eyes. He seems so upset. I have to keep calm and reasonable, but I'm afraid that he'll be mad at me forever. "Honor," he said. Seeing his face, I begin to understand what that very complicated word means. I can see in Aba's eyes that he's angry and ashamed at the same time. All these cameras pointed at him . . . I'm so furious at him, but I can't help feeling sorry for him, too. The respect of other men—that's so important here.

"What a mob scene!" exclaims a security guard. "The courtroom has never been so full."

There is a fresh barrage of camera flashes: someone important has arrived. It's Mohammad al-Ghazi, the chief justice of the tribunal. I can identify him thanks to his white turban, knotted behind his head. He has a thin mustache and a short beard, wears a gray jacket over his white tunic, and proudly displays his *jambia* at his waist.

I follow the judge's every move; I don't take my eyes off him for a second. I watch him sit down behind his raised desk, now cluttered with the microphones of radio and TV stations. I watch him set his files down in front of him. You'd think he was the president of the republic getting ready to speak. Judge Abdo joins him, sitting down in the chair next to him. Fortunately, they're here to support me. I still can't believe my eyes.

"In the name of God, the Almighty and Merciful, I declare this court open," announces al-Ghazi, inviting us to approach the bench.

Shada motions for me to follow her. To our left, Aba and the monster also move forward. I sense the crowd seething behind us. A part of me feels incredibly strong, but I have no control over the rest of me, which would give anything, right at this moment, to be a tiny mouse. Arms crossed, I try to hold on.

Then it's Judge Abdo's turn to speak.

"Here we have the case of a little girl who was

married without her consent. Once the marriage contract was signed without her knowledge, she was taken away by force into the province of Hajja. There, her husband sexually abused her, when she hadn't even reached the age of puberty and was not ready for sexual relations. Not only did he abuse her, but he also struck and insulted her. She has come here today to ask for a divorce."

The big moment is coming, the one I have been so anxious for, the moment when the guilty are punished. As in school, when the teacher would send us to the corner. I only hope I win against the monster. I hope *he* will accept the divorce.

Mohammad al-Ghazi raps the desk a few times with a small wooden hammer.

"Listen to me carefully," he tells the repulsive creature I hate more than anything. "You married this little girl two months ago, you slept with her, you struck her. Is that true, yes or no?"

The monster blinks, then replies, "No, it isn't true! She and her father agreed to this marriage."

Did I hear correctly? How can he say . . . ? What a liar! I detest him!

"Did you sleep with her? Did you sleep with her?" repeats Ghazi.

A heavy silence falls in the courtroom.

"No!"

"Did you hit her?"

"No. I was never violent with her."

I clutch at Shada's coat. How can he be so sure of himself, with his yellow teeth, his sneering smile, and his messy hair? How can he tell so many lies so easily? I can't let him get away with this. I have to say something.

"He's lying!"

The judge jots a few things down, then turns to my father.

"Did you agree to this marriage?"

"Yes."

"How old is your daughter?"

"My daughter is thirteen."

Thirteen? No one ever told me I was thirteen. Since when have I been that old? I thought I was nine or ten at the most! I wring my hands, trying to calm down, and I listen.

"I married off my daughter because I was afraid," continues my father. "I was afraid."

His eyes are bloodshot. Afraid? Of what?

"I married her off for fear she would be stolen, like her two older sisters," he says, shaking his fists over his head. "A man already took two of my daughters! He kidnapped them. That's already too much to bear. Today he is in prison."

I don't really understand what he's talking about.

His answers are vague and complicated, and the judge's questions are increasingly incomprehensible. I'm too young to unravel all this nonsense. Words, words, and more words. Quiet at first, then hard, like stones hurled at a wall, and shattering. The rhythm gradually quickens; voices are raised; I hear the accused men defend themselves. The uproar in the room grows louder as my heart pounds faster. The monster whispers something to Mohammad al-Ghazi, who raps for silence.

"At the husband's request, these proceedings will continue *in camera*," he announces.

He motions for us to follow him into another room, away from the public. I feel calmer away from the crowd—after all, these matters are very personal. But the questions begin again behind closed doors. I must bear up.

"Faez Ali Thamer, did you consummate the marriage, yes or no?" asks the judge.

I hold my breath.

"Yes," admits the monster. "But I was gentle with her, I was careful. I did not beat her."

His answer is like a slap in the face, reminding me of all those other slaps, the insults, the suffering. *What, he didn't beat you?* says my little inner voice. *And all those bruises on your arms, those tears of pain? You must fight back.*

"That's not true!" I yell, beside myself with anger.

Everyone turns to look at me. But I'm the first to be astonished at my outburst, which isn't at all like me.

After that, everything happens quickly. The monster is flushed with anger. *He* says that my father betrayed him by lying about my age. Then Aba becomes furious and says *he* had agreed to wait until I was older before touching me. At that point, the monster announces that *he* is ready to accept the divorce, but on one condition: my father must pay back my bride-price. And Aba snaps back that he was never paid anything at all. It's like a marketplace! How much? When? How? Who's telling the truth? Who's telling lies? Someone suggests that 50,000 rials (about 250 dollars) be paid to my husband, if that would allow the case to be closed. It would take a workman four months to earn that much money. I'm lost. Will everyone just finish up this business and leave me alone, once and for all? I've had enough of these grown-up quarrels that make children suffer. Stop!

In the end, I am saved by the judge's verdict.

"The divorce is granted," he announces.

The divorce is granted! I can't believe my ears. How

curious, this sudden desire to run and scream to express my joy. I'm so happy that I don't even pay attention to the fact that the judge has just announced that my father and the monster will be released, without even a fine to be paid or a signed promise of good conduct. For the moment, I just want to fully enjoy my regained freedom.

Leaving the small room, I find the crowd still waiting, noisier than ever.

"Say a few words for the cameras, just a few words!" shouts a journalist.

People crowd around to see me, applauding. I hear a great wave of congratulations on all sides: *"Mabrouk!"*

Behind me, I hear someone murmur that I must certainly be the youngest divorcée in the world.

Then come the gifts: a man who says he represents a Saudi benefactor who has been moved by my story slips a bundle of 150,000 rials into my hand. That's almost 750 dollars! I've never seen so much money.

"This girl is a heroine; she deserves a reward," he exclaims. Another man talks about an Iraqi woman who wants to give me some gold.

I'm surrounded by crackling flashbulbs, and by reporters. One of my uncles stands up from a bench and calls out to Shada: "You've sullied the reputation of our family! You have stained our honor!"

Turning to me, Shada whispers, "He's just babbling."

She takes my hand and leads me away. After all, I have nothing more to fear from my uncle, since I won. I won—I'm divorced! And the marriage—gone for good. It's peculiar, this feeling of lightness, of returning suddenly to my childhood.

"Khaleh Shada?"

"Yes, Nujood?"

"I'd like some new toys! I feel like eating chocolate and cakes!"

Shada gives me a big smile.

8

The Birthday

So this is what happiness is. Ever since I left the courthouse a few hours ago, something wonderful has been happening to me. In the street, the din of the traffic jams has never seemed so sweet to me. When we passed a grocery store just now, I thought about having a big ice-cream cone, and I told myself, *I bet I could eat a second one, and even a third. . . .* Spotting a cat in the distance, I felt like running over to pet it. My eyes are shining, as if they were discovering for the first time the slightest bits of beauty in being alive. I feel happy. This is the best day of my life.

"How do I look, Shada?"

"Beautiful, simply beautiful."

To celebrate my victory, Shada gave me some brand-new clothes. In my new pink sweatshirt and my pre-faded blue jeans embroidered with colorful butterflies, I feel like a new Nujood. My long, curly hair is pinned up in a twist and set off with a green ribbon, and I'm feeling fine. Especially since I have the right to take off my black veil, so now everyone can compliment me on my hair!

We have an appointment at the *Yemen Times* with Hamed and a few other journalists. The building is impressive, three stories high, with a uniformed guard watching everyone who comes and goes through the main door, like the guards at the villas of the chic neighborhoods in Sana'a that I love to draw. A little dizzy with emotion, I hold on to the wooden railing as I climb the marble steps of the big staircase. The windows are so clean that the sunshine makes little yellow circles on the white walls, and there's a nice smell of floor wax in the air.

On the second floor, Nadia, the editor in chief of the *Yemen Times*, welcomes me with a hug. I would never have imagined that a woman could manage a newspaper. How can her husband accept that? Seeing my astonishment, Nadia laughs gaily.

"Come, follow me."

In her large, bright office, Nadia pushes open a door—to a child's room, where the floor is strewn with toys and little cushions.

"This is my daughter's room," she explains. "Sometimes I bring her along with me to the paper. That way, I can be a mama *and* keep working."

A room just for her daughter! The universe that is opening up to me is so different from mine. I almost have the impression that I've landed on another planet. It's intimidating—and fascinating.

And the surprises are just beginning. When Nadia invites me to follow her to what she calls the editorial room, I am dumbfounded to discover that most of the journalists are women. Some wear black from head to toe, raising their *niqab*s only to take a sip of tea. Others wear orange or red scarves, which allow a few blond curls to escape and complement their blue eyes and milk-white skin. These women wear polish on their long fingernails, and they speak Arabic with a strange accent. They must be foreigners (Americans, or Germans?), perhaps with Yemeni husbands. They have certainly studied long years at universities to earn their positions here. And like Shada, they probably drive their own cars when they come to work.

I imagine them drinking coffee and smoking cigarettes, like the women on television. Maybe they even wear lipstick when they go out to dinner downtown. One of them is on the phone; it must be a very important call. I listen and let myself drift along on her melodious language. English, I suppose. One day, I'm going to speak English, too.

Watching them is endlessly interesting: I'm particularly struck by their ability to concentrate while they tap away on machines with their eyes glued to the screens I see atop every desk of pale wood. To be able to work while watching *Tom and Jerry*—what talent, and what luxury!

"Nujood, those are computers," Hamed exclaims, amused by my enthusiasm.

"They're what?"

"Computers! Machines connected to keyboards that allow you to write articles and send letters. You can even store photos in them."

Machines that let you write letters and keep photos? These women are not only attractive, but also very modern. I try to see myself in their place in ten or twenty years, with shiny nails, holding a pen. I wouldn't mind being a journalist. Or a lawyer. Or maybe both? With my computer, I would send letters to Hamed and Shada. I would work hard, that's for sure, and I would have a job that would allow me to help people in trouble and bring them a better life.

My tour of the premises ends at the conference room, "Where we hold all our important events," Nadia tells me.

A man shouts, "Bravo, Nujood!"

A chorus of voices then cheers, "Nujood won, Nujood won!"

When I go through the big door I see some thirty faces, all looking at me with eager eyes, and applause rings through the room. Nods, smiles, and blown kisses welcome me, and I pinch my right hand to convince myself I'm not dreaming. Yes, it's all real, and today, the "important event" is me.

I'm showered with gifts. First, Hamed hands me an enormous stuffed red bear, so tall it comes almost to my shoulders. On its round tummy there's a large heart decorated with letters I can't read.

"It's English writing. It means, 'I love you,' " Hamed says.

I don't even know which way to turn with all the packages being handed to me from every side. I untie the ribbons one by one, and it's surprise after surprise: a little battery-powered piano, colored pencils, pads of drawing paper, and a Fulla doll, like the ones in Judge Abdel Wahed's house.

When I try to find words to express my gratitude, only one comes to mind: "*Shokran!* Thank you!"

And I give everyone a big smile.

Then Nadia invites me to cut a cake: it's chocolate, my favorite flavor, with five red cherries on top. And suddenly I remember one of my escapades on

Hayle Avenue, with Mona. How many times, with my nose pressed to the boutique windows, had I dreamed about a wedding celebration with presents and evening gowns? Things hadn't turned out that way.

Compared to dreams, reality can be truly cruel. But it can also come up with beautiful surprises.

Today I finally understand the meaning of the word *party*. If it were a dessert, it would be sugary, and crunchy, perhaps with something soft inside, like my favorite coconut candies.

Holding my big stuffed bear in my arms, I announce, "A divorce party—that's really better than a wedding party!"

"And on this very special occasion, what can we sing for you, Nujood?" asks Nadia.

"I don't know."

While I hesitate, Shada has an idea: "Why don't we sing 'Happy Birthday'?"

"Happy 'birthday'? What's a birthday?" I ask, a little confused.

"A birthday is when people celebrate the day someone was born."

"All right, but there's a problem."

"What do you mean?"

"It's just that I don't know when I was born."

"Well, then, from now on, today will be your birthday!" exclaims Shada.

The room fills with applause.

"Happy birthday, Nujood! Happy birthday!"

I feel like laughing and laughing. It's so simple to be happy, when you're among friends.

9

Mona

June 2008

My divorce has changed my life. I don't cry anymore. My bad dreams are starting to go away. I feel stronger, as if all these ordeals have toughened me. When I go out in the street, sometimes women in the neighborhood call to me, congratulating me and shouting *"Mabrouk!"*—a word once tainted by evil memories, but which I now like to hear again. And shouted by women I don't even know! I blush, but deep down I'm so proud.

Since I always keep my ears open, I'm even managing to better understand all the family mysteries swirling around my sisters and brothers—especially around Mona. Her story is like a complicated puzzle that puts itself together piece by piece. . . .

"Wait for me, I'm coming with you," Mona yells, running after the car.

Today two women have come to my home to see me: a foreign journalist and Eman, a women's rights activist. I recently left my uncle's house and returned to live with my parents, because in my country, there are no shelters for girls who are the victims of family violence. It's good to be home, and although I am indeed still angry at Aba, he himself has reason to resent what I did. Actually, we all seem to be pretending to have forgotten what happened. For the moment, it's better that way.

My parents have just moved to a new neighborhood, Dares, which lies along the road to the airport. Our little house has only two small rooms, decorated with simple cushions leaning against the walls. At night, the noise of the airplanes approaching to land often wakes us up, but at least I know that here I can keep an eye on Haïfa, to protect her. If anyone dares to come ask for her hand, I will immediately protest. I'll say, "No! It's forbidden!" And if no one listens to me, I'll call the police. In my pocket I preciously guard the telephone Hamed gave me, a shiny new cell phone like Shada's, so that I can call her at any time.

Mohammad, my big brother, is not pleased. Ever since the session in court, he often yells at Haïfa and me. He takes my father aside, telling him that all this publicity about our family isn't good for our reputation. He's jealous, I'm sure of that: it shows in the faces he makes every time a reporter comes knocking at our door. To my utter amazement, my story has traveled swiftly around the globe, and every week new journalists arrive from lands with names as exotic as France, Italy, or even America. Just to see me!

"With all these foreigners lurking in the neighborhood, Nujood is drawing shame to our family," my brother grumbles to Eman as soon as she arrives.

"She's the one who ought to be ashamed of you!" Eman shoots back.

Bravo, Eman! says my little voice. Mohammad doesn't quite know what to say, so he sulks off to a corner of the main room, while I hurry to put on my black scarf before he can forbid me from going out. I've never been to the amusement park, and Eman has promised to take us there—an adventure not to be missed! I grab Haïfa's hand to take her with me, so she won't be left to face Mohammad's anger by herself. I will never abandon Haïfa, my protégée. We are already in the car when Mona catches up with us, galloping along in her coat and *niqab*.

"Mohammad ordered me to accompany you," she gasps.

Mona seems distressed about something, but insistent, saying that she won't let us leave without her. We realize that we had better do as our older brother says. Mona slips into the front seat next to the driver. I think I understand what's going on: annoyed, Mohammad has surely decided to take revenge by sending Mona to spy on me. But I quickly discover that poor Mona has other intentions.

After we set out, Mona announces that before we go to the park, she would like to make a detour through our old neighborhood, Al-Qa. What a strange idea! Has Mohammad sent her on some special mission? Bewildered by Mona's insistence, Eman finally agrees and, making our way back to Al-Qa, we arrive in front of a mosque.

"Stop!" Mona tells the driver.

I've never seen her so upset. The car brakes suddenly. On the front steps of the mosque, a hand emerging from a long, shabby black veil reaches out to passersby, hungry for the slightest little coin. The other hand cups the cheek of a sleeping little girl in a stained, too-small dress, her hair a mass of tangles.

"It's Monira!" I shout.

Monira, Mona's daughter, my tiny niece! But what is she doing here, in the arms of a beggar woman without a face, completely swathed in black?

"Ever since my husband went to prison, my mother-in-law has insisted on having custody of

Monira," Mona murmurs, to everyone's astonishment. "She says that with a child, it's easier to soften the hearts of passersby."

I'm openmouthed. Monira, that delicate little doll, condemned to beg in the arms of Mona's ragged mother-in-law? Mona's husband, behind bars? What's going on? So he's the man in prison, the one Aba mentioned in the courtroom. I can see that Mona is too busy tenderly kissing her daughter, whom she has torn from her veiled exhibitor, to give us any explanations.

"I miss her so much. I'll bring her back to you, I promise," I hear her say to the old woman in black, before she plunges back into the car, cradling her three-year-old in her arms.

The car suddenly smells musty; Monira is so filthy that we have trouble telling what color shoes she's wearing.

The car door slams and off we go. Tiny Monira is so happy to see her mother and aunts again that we almost forget our shock at having found her in such miserable circumstances.

The driver heads for the southwest quarter of the city. Along the way we pass another mosque, this one under construction, and it's so grand, so magnificent, that it looks like a castle. I peer out the window, admiring the six giant minarets.

For the moment, though, my thoughts are focused on Mona. When we reach the park, she slowly opens her heart to us.

"It's a long story," she says and sighs, allowing Monira to go hide behind a bush, chaperoned by Haïfa.

The three women are all sitting cross-legged under a tree, with Eman and the journalist facing Mona as I listen in.

"Mohammad, my husband, was put in prison a few weeks before Nujood's marriage. He had been found in our oldest sister Jamila's bedroom. I'd been having my suspicions for some time, and finally, for my peace of mind, I had some people come who caught them red-handed, and the situation quickly turned ugly. The police came and took Mohammad and Jamila away, and they've been languishing in prison ever since. I don't know for how long."

Mona bows her head, and I stare at her, dazed, not really knowing what to say. It's hard for me to grasp the seriousness of what she's telling us, but it all seems terrible.

"In Yemen," Eman murmurs, "adultery is a crime punishable by death."

"Yes, I know," Mona replies. "That's surely why

Mohammad is pressuring me to sign a paper that will allow the affair to be covered up. I am to pretend that we were divorced before his arrest. I refuse to visit him in prison, but that's the message he has sent to me. I won't give in! He made me suffer so much."

Mona hasn't ever been this talkative before; as she speaks, her hands are never still, and her eyes blaze in the little window of her *niqab*, which hides the rest of her face. My heart is in my throat as I listen to her quavering voice. And then, out of the blue, all of us burst into crazy laughter: crouching behind that bush, Monira has just pulled down her panties, and a thin yellow stream waters the sun-scorched grass.

"Monira!" Mona says scoldingly, returning to her motherly role while a smile plays around her lips. But her eyes soon grow sad again. "Monira, my dear one. I'll be forced to bring up my two children alone—providing, of course, that my mother-in-law allows me to see them. As for Mohammad, he was never a good father. And he wasn't a good husband, either."

After a pause, Mona takes up her tale again.

"I wasn't much older than Nujood when I was forced to marry him. Our family and I were living happy days in Khardji, until that black hour when everything fell apart."

Slowly, I creep closer to hear better; I think I've already heard too much for my age, but now I definitely want to hear the end of this story. She's my sister, after all, and strangely enough, I feel responsible for her.

"Omma had just left for Sana'a to seek emergency medical treatment for her serious health problems—some doctors had advised her to consult a specialist in the capital. As usual, Aba had left early to see to his herd. I was alone in the house with my little brothers and Nujood, who was only a baby. A young man I didn't know came to the house; he must have been about thirty. He began making advances toward me, and no matter how hard I tried to chase him away, he managed to push me into the bedroom. I fought back, I screamed, I yelled 'No!' but—" She breaks off, then says, "When Aba came home, it was too late. Everything had happened too quickly."

I can't believe this! Poor Mona—she, too . . . Her constant gloom, that depressed look in her eyes, the bursts of hysterical laughter—so *this* is why.

"Aba was furious. He immediately raised the alarm to find out what had happened, and began accusing the villagers of a plot, but none of our neighbors wanted to listen. Informed of the business, the village sheikh married us hastily, before rumors could spread from house to house and valley to valley. In the name of honor! He said it was best to stamp out such rumors right away.

"No one ever asked me what I thought. They stuck a blue dress on me, and by the next day I was his wife. Meanwhile, Omma had returned to the village; she raised her hands to heaven, blaming herself for ever having left. Aba was ashamed, and wanted revenge, saying that the neighbors were responsible, that someone had certainly meant to harm him by attacking his children. He felt humiliated, betrayed. One evening, everyone gathered to talk things over, and the discussion grew heated. They began to trade insults; *jambia*s were drawn. A little later—that evening or the next day, I no longer remember very well—the neighbors came back with revolvers. They threatened us, ordering us to get out of the village right away. My parents left for Sana'a. My husband and I went to hide somewhere else for a few weeks, before finally rejoining the family in the capital."

I'm shaking inside. That hurried departure for Sana'a, my father's anger, Mona's sadness, her obsessive attention to me: now I understand.

"Years later, when our father told us that Nujood was going to be married, I felt sick about it. I kept begging him to think it over, telling him that Nujood was too young, but he wouldn't listen. He said that once she was married, she would be protected from kidnappers and the men always hanging around our neighborhood. He'd already had enough problems, he argued, because of me and Jamila. When the men of the family gathered to sign the marriage contract, they even talked about having a *sighar*, the traditional 'marriage exchange,' to wed the new husband's sister to my brother Fares, if he ever returned from Saudi Arabia.

"The evening of Nujood's wedding, I couldn't help crying when I saw her, lost in that dress, far too big for her. She was much too young! Hoping to protect her, I even went to talk to her husband. I made him swear before God not to touch her, to wait until she reached puberty, to let her play with children her age. 'It's a promise,' he said. But he didn't keep his word. He's a criminal! Men are all criminals. Never listen to them. Never, never."

I can't take my eyes off Mona's *niqab*. How I would love, at this very moment, to see the slightest bit of her face, hidden behind that black net, and the tears I imagine are streaming down her cheeks.

I'm ashamed of having suspected her of wanting to spy on us. If only I'd known! All that suffering, for so many years, endured without a protest or complaint, never raising her voice or taking refuge under a sheltering wing. Mona, my big sister, the prisoner of a fate even more tragic than mine, trapped in a maze of troubles. Her childhood was stolen from her, as mine was from me, but I now understand that, unlike Mona, I've had the strength to rebel against my fate, and the good fortune to find help.

"Mona! Nujood! Look at us! Watch us!"

Looking up, we see Haïfa sitting on a swing, with little Monira wedged between her knees, bubbling with laughter. Mona goes over to them, and I follow her. The swing next to the girls is empty.

"Nujood, help me fly away," she says.

Mona sits on the swing. I climb up behind her, placing a foot on each end of the wooden seat, and I grab the ropes on either side. Pumping with my legs, I start the seat swinging backward and forward, backward and forward, more and more quickly.

"Faster, Nujood, faster!" Mona shouts excitedly.

I feel the wind in my face, so cool and fresh. Mona laughs, the first time in a long while that she has laughed so lightheartedly. And this is the first time we've ever been on a swing together—I feel like a feather on the wind. It's so good, recovering this feeling of innocence.

"Omma's flying! Omma's flying!" Monira giggles from the swing next to ours.

Mona's yelping with joy. She doesn't want to stop.

After a few minutes, my scarf blows loose in the wind, and for once, I don't rush to readjust it. My hair tumbles down around my shoulders, rippling in the breeze. I feel free. Free!

10

The Return of Fares

August 2008

I've eaten a "bizza." That was a few days ago, in a very modern restaurant where the waiters all wore caps and shouted their orders into a microphone.

The bizza tasted so strange! It crunches under your teeth, like a big *khobz* flatbread, with lots of good things to eat on top: tomatoes, corn, chicken, olives. At the table next to us, there were ladies wearing scarves who looked like the women in the *Yemen Times* offices. They were very stylish, and even used a knife and fork to bring the pieces of bizza to their mouths.

I tried to imitate them, cutting my slice the same way. At first it wasn't easy; I got bizza everywhere. As for Haïfa, she saw a girl empty a bottle of spicy tomato sauce over her plate, so she wanted to try that, too. Except that, from the first mouthful, her throat was on fire and her eyes got all red! Luckily, one of the waiters finally left his mic to bring her a big bottle of water.

Now we have a new game: when we help Omma prepare meals, we pretend we're customers in a "bizzeria" who've come to choose their favorite dishes.

"How may I help you?" asks Haïfa, laying out the *sofrah* in our main room.

"Let's see, today, I think I'll have a cheese bizza."

Actually, I say *cheese* because when I rummaged through our pantry bag, I realized that that's all we have left to eat. Too bad; we'll cope.

"Come to the table," announces Haïfa, inviting the rest of the family to join us.

We've barely begun to eat, though, when someone knocks on our front door.

"Nujood, are you expecting more reporters?" Mohammad asks me suspiciously.

"No, not today."

"Then perhaps it's the water truck, to fill the cistern. But he usually comes in the morning."

Frowning, Mohammad gets to his feet, still chewing his mouthful of bread, and hurries to the front door. Who could be visiting us at this hour, in this stifling August heat? During very hot weather, visitors usually come at the end of the day.

Mohammad's cry startles us all.

"Fares!" he shouts. "Fares has come back!"

I feel faint. Fares, my beloved brother, whom I haven't seen in four years! Supporting herself against the wall with trembling hands, our mother staggers to the front door, and we're all close behind her, with little Rawdha trying to sneak ahead of us by slipping between our legs. Our tiny hall has never seemed so long.

The young man at the door has a gaunt face and deeply tanned skin; how he has changed! Tall and thin, Fares is no longer the adolescent in the photo I've studied so often, down to the slightest details. Now I must look way up to observe him closely. His eyes have a harder look, and his forehead bears a few dark creases, like Aba's. He has become a man.

"Fares! Fares! Fares!" moans our mother, clinging to his white tunic, hugging him tightly.

"We've missed you so much," I tell him, when it's my turn to kiss him.

Ramrod straight, Fares is silent. He seems exhausted; his eyes are empty, almost sad. Where has it gone, the ebullience that suited him so well?

"Fares, Fares!" Rawdha sings like a robot, without really understanding that this tall gentleman is her big brother, who left our home when she was still nothing but a little bitty baby.

ϫϫϫ

Since that short phone call from Saudi Arabia, two years after his flight, we hadn't heard a thing from him, until an unexpected call one evening, just last month. When Omma recognized his voice on the other end of the line, she shrieked with joy. Then we'd all torn the phone from her hands, one after another, to listen to him. He'd seemed distant, very far away, but it had warmed my heart to know he was alive.

"Are things going well for you, over there?" our father had hastened to ask, his voice cracking, on the verge of tears.

Aba wanted to know everything from Fares: For whom was he working? Did he like it there? Was he earning a good living? In answer, my brother had simply repeated the same question several times, as if possessed: "And *you*, how are *you*?" Then he told us, "I'm very worried about my family. I've heard things. Please tell me that everything's all right."

And he *was* worried—you could hear it in his voice. He explained to us that over there, rumours were circulating about our family. All the way out there, in Saudi Arabia, so remote that I couldn't even find it on a map! Yemeni travelers had told Fares that we'd had some problems, but they hadn't given him any details. And then one day Fares had seen a photo of our father and me in a local paper. But after years of playing hooky—he'd abandoned school at the end of the first year—he was simply incapable of reading the article beneath the picture, so that mysterious story had kept tormenting his mind, until he could no longer sleep.

Rumors carried by travelers, a photo in a Saudi paper: the news of my divorce had indeed traveled beyond my country's borders. At Fares's insistence, Aba quickly filled him in on what had happened in the past few months.

"Now I understand a little better," my brother said.

"Fares, my son, please, come home!" our mother had begged him, sniffling.

"I can't, I have work to do," he'd replied, and then the line had gone dead.

The call must have lasted about ten minutes, but that was enough to plunge Omma back into utter despair. She had recovered her taste for life after my divorce, but now she flew off the handle at the slightest thing. She wanted to see her son again, to smell him, to touch him. She simply couldn't bear seeing our family threatened anymore—some of us bolting, others being carried off. Why did fate always persecute her? Hadn't she, too, the right to be just a little bit happy, like other mamas?

Her nightmares returned. Fearing that Fares had

decided to abandon his family for good and had called just to ease his conscience, she felt she would never see him again. Her insomnia came back to plague her at night, and my heart broke to see her suffer. My divorce had opened my eyes about many things, making me more sensitive to the unhappiness of others.

And now, on this hot, oppressive day, my Fares has returned. A Fares much calmer and quieter than the one I remember, but those bushy eyebrows and that curly hair could belong only to my brother. I want to know everything about him. Does his boss treat him well? Has he made new friends in Saudi Arabia? And hey—surely they must eat good bizzas over there?

Refusing to let go of him, our mother pulls him by the arm into our second room. Fares isn't saying much; slowly, he takes off his shoes before collapsing onto a cushion. I don't take my eyes off him. In a flash, Omma brings him a glass of *chaï*, hot tea, from which he takes a few quick swallows.

"So, tell us a little," Aba urges him.

Fares sets his glass down on the *sofrah*.

"In four years, I wasn't able to save up a thing. I'm so sorry. If only I'd known," he murmurs, bowing his head.

Silence falls in the room. Then my brother's face relaxes a little, and a faint smile appears.

"You remember, Aba? I was so angry at you, that day, for having yelled at me when I came home empty-handed after going to beg some bread from the baker. I was eaten up by shame; I'd had enough of scrounging left and right for bits of change. I dreamed of new clothes, like all boys my age, but at home we had barely enough to buy food. The next day I woke up with the crazy desire to depend on no one but myself. I wanted to succeed, to earn money with a decent job, and buy myself the clothes I wanted. So I left, resolving not to return here until the day when my pockets were stuffed with money."

Fares pauses for a sip of tea.

"In the neighborhood there were people who talked about the chance to travel to Saudi Arabia. They said that over there a man can earn his living, and even send money back home to help his family. That was exactly what I needed. I wanted to try that adventure; I was full of ambition and had nothing to lose. I was young, thoughtless; I never imagined how hard things would be.

"It took me four days to reach Saudi Arabia. First I took a share taxi north to Sa'ada. The road to the city was full of army checkpoints, and I began to realize that the trip would be long and difficult. In

Sa'ada, I met a 'passer,' who offered to get me over the border for five thousand rials, about twenty-five dollars. That was expensive, but given my situation, I wasn't about to turn back. At least the man knew his business; he said he would use paths that would outsmart the border guards. Since I didn't have any identification papers on me, I decided to rely on him."

"We were so worried!" exclaims Aba. "We thought you'd disappeared for good."

Absorbed in his memories, Fares simply goes on with his story.

"We crossed the border on foot in the middle of the night. I have never been so scared in my life. Along the way, I encountered other Yemenis, some of them younger than I was. Like me, they didn't really know what awaited them on the other side, and had only one thought: to make their fortunes. It was walking through the darkness that made me understand the real risk I was taking. If I'd been caught by soldiers, they would have immediately sent me back to Sana'a.

"My relief at crossing the border was quickly overwhelmed by my confusion: Now what? Where should I go? It was the first time I'd ever set foot in a foreign land. Tired, I walked on until I reached the outskirts of the town of Khamiss Mousheid. What a disappointment! That part of Saudi Arabia is no better than Sana'a. A man from whom I had asked directions offered to put me up for the night. He lived out in the countryside with his wife and children.

"The next day, when he offered me a job, I accepted right away. I truly had no other choice. He raised sheep, and put me in charge of a herd of six hundred animals. I had to take them out to pasture every day, with the help of one other shepherd, who was from the Sudan. I worked twelve hours a day, from six in the morning until six in the evening. At night I shared my room with the Sudanese, in a tiny stone house in the middle of nowhere, furnished with only two little mattresses. There was no television, no refrigerator, no toilet, no air-conditioning. I lost all my illusions."

Fares pauses again, swallowing hard; his voice is growing hoarse, probably from fatigue after his journey.

"From then on, it was one disappointment after another. The boss grew more demanding every day. We had to feed the animals, water them, take them out into the fields. The workdays kept getting longer. It took me a month to realize how precarious my position was, when I received my salary for the first time: two hundred Saudi rials, a little over fifty dollars for thirty days' work, enough to buy myself some candy at the corner store—which belonged, strangely enough, to my boss.

"I was shaken. I figured out that I would have to work for at least a year to amass the necessary money to come home to Sana'a. I didn't have enough to phone you. Besides, I was too proud to admit my failure. The first time I called you, it was only to make you believe that all was well. The second time, two years later, it was because I was so worried."

He bows his head, and heaves a deep sigh.

"Once I'd hung up the phone, I couldn't help thinking about Omma's tears on the other end of the line. I couldn't sleep at night for thinking about them. I counted every last bit of my money: I had just enough to return to Sana'a. One morning last week, I went to tell my boss good-bye. I'd made up my mind: it was time to go home."

"And now what do you plan on doing?" asks Mohammad.

"Well, I'll do what the others do. I'll sell chewing gum in the street," replies Fares resignedly.

How he has changed! Fares, once so ambitious, today seems ready to accept defeat. I can still see his impudent expression when he stood up to Aba, like a colored drawing I would have thought could never be erased. I remember his cheekiness, which exasperated Aba but gave me a good laugh. If he had been with us at the bizzeria the other day, he would have been the first to make airplanes from the restaurant's paper napkins, and wing them over to the next table. It was in thinking about his impetuous energy that I'd found the strength, in April, to run away to the courthouse. His escape had given me the courage to fly with my own wings. I feel I owe him something.

Fares, beaten, no—that isn't like him. I would never have imagined that he would give up. It makes me sick at heart. One day I must manage to help him in turn. I don't really know how, but in the end, I'll find a way.

11

When I Become
a Lawyer . . .

September 16, 2008

The wind is blowing in Sana'a, the wind at summer's end that heralds the return of cool evenings and the first sprinkles of rain. Once again, my little brothers and sisters will be able to play in the puddles with the other neighborhood children. Outdoors, the trees will soon turn yellow, and the blanket peddlers will reappear at the intersections.

For me, this wind is finally a back-to-school wind, the moment I have so longed for. I had trouble sleeping last night; before dropping off, I was careful to fill my new brown cloth backpack with brand-new notebooks. On a scrap of paper, I practiced writing my name, and Malak's name, too. I thought a lot about my former classmate, but unfortunately I'm registered at a different school, so I won't see her.

In my dreams I saw crisp blank notebooks, colored pencils, and lots of girls my age all around me. My nightmares finally stopped a few weeks ago; I no longer wake up in a sweat, weeping, my mouth dry, thinking about the door bursting open and the oil lamp being knocked over. Instead, I've been dreaming about school, like a wish you say boldly out loud, hoping it will finally come true.

When I opened my eyes this morning, the first thing I felt was my heart beating excitedly. Then I tiptoed off to brush my teeth and comb my hair. The other women and girls of the family were still sleeping, lying in a row on the floor in the little back room. Next door, in the main room where the men sleep, flies were buzzing around. Before I put on my new schoolgirl's uniform—a long green dress and a white scarf—I ran cool water over my face for a long time.

"Haïfa, rise and shine, we'll be late!"

Her hair every which way, half her face creased by the pillow, my little sister has trouble waking up. While I dash to the door to wait for the taxi, Omma helps her dress and put on her shoes. Now she can't find her head scarf. Never mind, she'll wear a different one—a bit stained, it's true, but we'll do better tomorrow. The driver is already here, sitting behind the wheel. The international humanitarian association that is paying our school fees and moving expenses has sent him to be our "school bus."

"Are you ready?" he asks us.

"Yes."

"Well, let's go!"

Now my heart is really pounding. I grab my backpack and pull it proudly over my shoulders. Before climbing into the taxi, we kiss Omma, to whose dress little Rawdha is clinging as she waves bye-bye to us. Suddenly she spots some sheep trotting along in the distance and lets out a peal of laughter. Our little concrete house, at the very end of a no-exit dirt road, is behind a Coca-Cola factory and a field where half the land lies fallow, so shepherds bring their flocks there at daybreak.

Sitting side by side in the backseat, Haïfa and I smile conspiratorially at each other when we hear the engine start up. Without saying a word, we both know that at this moment we are insanely happy. And nervous. I've waited so long for the day when I could finally draw new pictures, learn Arabic, study the Koran and arithmetic. When I had to leave school last February, I knew how to count to a hundred. Now I want to learn to count to a million!

My nose pressed to the window, I glance up at the

pure blue sky. This morning, the wind has chased away every cloud. The streets are astonishingly empty; the shopkeepers haven't raised their corrugated-iron curtains yet. For once, the old neighbor who constantly complains about the stream of journalists coming to our door hasn't come out to spy on us from his front steps. The corner bakery is still closed, with no one waiting in line. Most unusually, this year classes are beginning around the same time as Ramadan, and half the city is still asleep.

This is the first time I am fasting between the morning and evening prayers, like the grown-ups. For a few days at the beginning it wasn't easy, especially because of the heat that dries out your throat and makes you very thirsty, and I even thought I might pass out, but I've quickly learned to love this long month of reflection and celebration, during which our lives differ from the normal routines we follow the rest of the year. When the sun dips behind the houses in late afternoon, we eat things suitable for Ramadan: dates, *shorba*—a barley soup—and *floris*—little turnovers of potatoes and meat. And we stay up late, sometimes until three in the morning! At night the restaurants are packed with people, and the neon signs for clothing and toy stores stay lighted for long hours. Downtown, not far from Bab al-Yemen, it's so crowded that it's almost impossible to move.

When I awoke this morning around five o'clock, for the first prayer of the day, I thanked God for not abandoning me these last few months. I asked him to help me remain in good health and have a successful second year in primary school. I also prayed for help for Aba and Omma, for them to earn some money so that my brothers can stop begging in the streets, and Fares can smile again the way he used to. If only school could be compulsory for all children; that would keep boys like him from being forced to hawk chewing gum at red lights. I also thought a lot about Jad, my grandfather; I miss him, but I told myself that up above, he must be proud of me.

The taxi has just turned onto the main avenue, the one leading to the airport. Once we've gone through the army checkpoint, we peel off to the right, passing several concrete houses whose flat roofs sport satellite dishes. Maybe one day there will be a television in our home, too. The driver presses a button and the rear windows open automatically. In the distance, I can hear girls singing, their voices growing louder as we drive along.

"Here we are," announces our chauffeur, parking in front of a big black iron gate.

The trip has taken barely five minutes. I feel a thrill of excitement and apprehension. Now the girls' song is so close that I recognize the words: an old nursery rhyme I must have learned last year. Behind this gate is my new school.

"Good morning, Nujood!"

Shada! What a surprise! I throw myself into her arms and hug her tightly. She made certain to come witness this great day. If only she knew how reassured I am to see a familiar face.

The gate opens onto a large graveled courtyard embraced on three sides by a gray-brick two-story building housing a dozen classrooms. All the girls wear the same green and white uniform that Haïfa and I have on. I don't know anyone, and it's intimidating. Shada introduces me to the principal, Njala Matri, a woman veiled in black, except for her eyes.

"*Kifalek*, Nujood? How are you?"

Her voice is both gentle and confident. She invites us to follow her to her office at the far end of the courtyard. A pot of plastic flowers sits on the red tablecloth of the conference table, and a large poster of President Ali Abdullah al-Saleh decorates the main wall. At a desk, a teacher sits typing on a computer keyboard. After closing the office door, Njala Matri lifts the *niqab* from her face. She's so pretty! She has blue-gray eyes and milk-white skin.

"Nujood, you are welcome here. This school is your home."

I'm beginning to relax a little. The principal explains to us that the school, which is financed by donations from local residents, accepts about twelve hundred students each year, and has between forty and fifty per class. Here, she insists, the women teachers listen to their girl pupils, who even have the right to speak to them after class if they feel the need to ask questions of a more personal nature.

Hearing that, I feel relieved. I had begun to believe that I would never manage to return to school. One teacher had even opposed my attendance at first.

"You understand, she's not a little girl like the others," this teacher had whispered to Shada when we'd first visited the school. "After all, she's had relations, you know, with a man. That might have an effect on her classmates."

Shada must have considered other offers, and very attractive ones, but in her opinion they were too extravagant: studies abroad financed by an international organization, or attendance at a private school in Sana'a. Was I really cut out for that? Was I ready to leave my family, especially Haïfa? No, not now. Not yet. So I chose the school in the nearby neighborhood of Rawdha, so that people would stop staring at me, so that I would be treated like everyone else, like my little sister.

"Well, hi there, Nujood! Oh, you are sooooooooo cute!"

Oops—not this time, I guess! A woman with blue eyes, perfect posture, and a mauve scarf awkwardly draped over her short hair has just appeared in the middle of the courtyard. Surrounded by schoolgirls, she's waving her hands around and talking loudly, but the words pouring out seem like gibberish. Must be a foreign language.

Shada explains to me that she works for *Glamour*, an important American women's magazine. She has come all the way to Yemen because of me. I'm going to have to tell my story again. Over and over. And once again, my face will freeze when we get to those personal questions I always find so painful to answer. And that anguish I try so hard to stifle will well up deep in my heart.

All of a sudden, the bell rings. Saved! Pointing with a stick, one of the teachers, Najmiya, signals to the girls to line up along the wall. I hurry to obey. Then she ushers my group into a classroom, where she invites us to sit down at the desks lined up there in two sections. I choose one next to a window: not up in the front of the room, nor all the way in the back, but in the third row, next to two new classmates whose first names I haven't yet learned. My eyes glued to the blackboard, I try to decipher the letters our teacher has just written in white chalk: *Ra-ma-dan Ka-rim*. Ramadan Karim! Happy Ramadan! Like a puzzle finally solved, the words slip back into place in my memory. And my racing heart returns to its normal beat.

While the teacher is encouraging us to recite the words of our national anthem, I suddenly focus on the rustle of turning pages. This is the true sound of school, found again at last.

For a moment, I think about a story the principal told Shada a little while ago.

"Last year, one of our thirteen-year-old pupils left school suddenly, without giving a reason. At first I thought she would be back. And then the weeks went by, but we never heard any news of her. Until the day a few months ago when I learned that the child had gotten married and had a baby. At thirteen!"

With the best of intentions, I'm sure, Njala Matri had been careful to whisper this to Shada so that I wouldn't hear her, but what she doesn't know is that

for the last few weeks I've been formulating a plan.
Yes; I've made up my mind. When I grow up, I'll be
a lawyer, like Shada, to defend other little girls like
me. If I can, I'll propose that the legal age for marriage be raised to eighteen. Or twenty. Or even
twenty-two! I will have to be strong and tenacious. I
must learn not to be afraid of looking men right in
the eye when I speak to them. In fact, one of these
days I'll have to get up enough courage to tell Aba
that I don't agree with him when he says that, after
all, the Prophet married Aïsha when she was only
nine years old. Like Shada, I will wear high heels,
and I will not cover my face. That *niqab*—you can't
breathe under it! But first things first: I will have to
do my homework well. I must be a good student, so
that I can hope to go to college and study law. If I
work hard, I'll get there.

Ever since I ran away to the courthouse, events have
moved so quickly that I haven't yet had a chance to
fully understand everything that has happened to
me. I will definitely need some time, and patience.
Shada has suggested more than once, actually, that I
see a doctor who she says could help me, and each
time I've decided to cancel the appointment at the

last minute. It's upsetting, isn't it, to go to a doctor you don't know? So Shada finally gave up.

It's true that at first I was eaten up with shame—shame, the fear of being different from other people, and a painful feeling of inferiority. I couldn't help having the strange notion that I'd been going through my ordeal all alone, that I'd been the anonymous victim of something no one else could understand.

But recently I've realized that my case was not unique. What happened to me and to that thirteen-year-old schoolgirl—no one talks much about those stories, but there are more of them than you might imagine. A few weeks ago Shada introduced me to Arwa and Rym, two girls who had just filed for divorce. When I saw them for the first time, I gave them big hugs, as if they'd been my sisters. Their stories had a huge impact on me. At nine, Arwa was forced by her father to marry a man twenty-five years older than she was, but after hearing about me on the television, she decided one morning to go for help to the hospital nearest her home, in the village of Jibla, to the south of Sana'a. Rym was twelve when her life was turned upside down by her parents' divorce. For revenge, her father married her off to a thirty-one-year-old cousin. After several attempts at suicide,

Rym found the courage to knock on the courthouse door.

I was proud to learn that my story had helped them find the means to defend themselves, and I feel responsible in a small way for their decisions to rebel against their husbands. Touched by their unhappiness, I empathized deeply with their suffering, and listening to them speak, I saw my misfortunes reflected in the mirror of theirs. I thought, *Khalass*—enough. Marriage was invented to make girls miserable. I will never get married again, not ever again. *Machi! Machtich!*

I often think about what happened to Mona. Life hasn't smiled on her, either. And a week ago, my big sister Jamila was finally released from prison. When she walked into our house, I threw my arms around her. What a surprise to see her again!

She had had to share her cell with criminals, even with women accused of killing their husbands. In our house, though, we aren't talking about such things, so as not to spoil Jamila's homecoming. And for the first time in a long while, it's true, our family is once again complete. After the joy of being reunited, however, the quarreling began again, and the other day my sisters had a spat. Although Mona had finally agreed to sign that famous paper to save Jamila, she couldn't help being angry at her, accusing her sister of having broken up her family. Nothing will ever be the same again between the two of them, and yet, all this trouble is the husband's fault. Sometimes I think that one day I will have to speak to Fares and make him promise that if he gets married, he will be the sweetest of husbands.

A plane crosses the sky, leaving behind a long white trail that puffs up as I watch it. Meanwhile, the plane goes on its way, and will surely land soon at the nearby airport. Perhaps it has come from France, or maybe Bahrain? Which of those two countries is closer to us, anyway? I'll have to ask Shada. One day I, too, will fly away in the sky, and I'll go to the far ends of the earth. It seems that at least three hundred people can fit into an airplane. A neighbor who just returned from Saudi Arabia told me that the inside of a plane looks like a huge living room, where you can read magazines while you order your meal on a tray. In the plane, he added, everyone eats with real cutlery, just like in the bizzeria!

The teacher's high-pitched voice finally rouses me from my reverie.

"Who would like to recite the Fatiha, the first

sura of the Koran?" she asks, addressing the entire class.

With an enthusiasm I haven't dared feel for a very long time, I quickly raise my hand, stretching high so that everyone can see me. It's strange; for once I haven't bothered to think something over before acting. I didn't ask myself what Aba would think, or what people might say behind my back. I, Nujood, ten years old—I have chosen to answer a question. And this choice is mine alone.

"Nujood?" says the teacher, turning to look at me. My eagerness has caught her eye.

Taking a deep breath, I launch myself from my seat, ramrod straight, and begin rummaging through my memory to find the verses of the Koran I learned last year.

In the Name of Allah, the Most Merciful,
the Most Compassionate.
Praise be to Allah, Lord of the Universe,
The Most Merciful, the Most Compassionate,
Sovereign of the Day of Judgment!
You alone we worship, and to You alone we turn for help.
Guide us to the straight path,
The path of those whom You have favored,
Not of those who have incurred Your wrath,
Nor of those who have gone astray.

A solemn silence now reigns in the classroom.

"Bravo, Nujood. May Allah protect you!" The teacher applauds, encouraging the other pupils to do the same. Then she looks over at the other side of the room, seeking a new candidate.

With a smile, I sit down again at my desk. Glancing around me, I can't help heaving a great sigh of relief. In my green and white uniform, I'm only one of fifty girls in this class. I am a pupil in the second year of primary school. I have just started classes again, like thousands of other little Yemeni girls. When I go home this afternoon, I will have homework to do, and drawings to make with colored pencils.

Today I finally feel that I've become a little girl again. A normal little girl. Like before. I'm just me.

Epilogue

Clinging tightly to Shada's hand in her pretty purple dress, Nujood flashes smiles on all sides. Her movements are shy, but she has a determined look in her eyes.

"Another shot!" yell the paparazzi.

On November 10, 2008, in New York City, the youngest divorcée in the world has just been named a Woman of the Year by *Glamour*. With all the gravitas of her ten years, she shares this unexpected honor with the film star Nicole Kidman, the American secretary of state Condoleezza Rice, and Senator Hillary Clinton, among others. That's quite a feat for this little Yemeni girl, this once anonymous victim who has suddenly become a heroine for our time, and who today aspires to return to a normal life, one she richly deserves.

Nujood has won. And she's proud of that. The thing that struck me immediately, when Nujood and I first met in June 2008, two months after her divorce, was precisely her self-confidence. It was as if her incredible struggle had made her grow up all at once, by casually stealing away the lovely innocence of childhood.

She'd sounded so grown-up when carefully explaining to me, over the phone, the slightest details of the route to take to find her unassuming little house, lost in the labyrinth of dusty streets in Dares, on the outskirts of Sana'a, the capital of Yemen.

When I arrived, she was waiting for me near a busy gas station, wrapped in a black veil, with her younger sister Haïfa by her side. "I'll be near the candy vendor," she had told me, betraying the sweet tooth of children her age. Almond-shaped eyes, a baby face, an angelic smile. Seemingly a girl like any other, who likes candy, dreams of having a big TV, and plays blindman's buff with her brothers and sisters. Deep down, however, she is a real little lady, matured by her ordeal, who smiles today to hear the congratulatory cries of *"Mabrouk!"* called out to her by the women of Sana'a when they recognize her as she passes by.

Husnia al-Kadri, the director of women's affairs at the University of Sana'a, confided to me not long ago that "Nujood's divorce kicked down a closed door."

Husnia al-Kadri was in charge of a recent study revealing that more than half the girls in Yemen get married before the age of eighteen.

Yes, it's true: Nujood's story carries a message of hope. In this country of the Arabian Peninsula, where the marriage of little girls draws on traditions that until now have seemed unshakable, her unbelievable act of bravery has encouraged other small voices to speak out against their husbands. After Nujood's day in court, two other girls—Arwa, nine years old, and Rym, twelve—also undertook the legal struggle to break their barbaric bonds of matrimony. In neighboring Saudi Arabia, one year after Nujood's historic court case, an eight-year-old Saudi girl married off by her father to a man in his fifties successfully sued for divorce—the first time such a thing has happened in that ultraconservative country.

In February 2009, the Yemeni parliament finally passed a new law raising the legal age of consent to seventeen for both boys and girls. In addition, in an attempt to prevent the formation of "overextended" families like Nujood's, who are often unable to care properly for their children, this law allows a man to marry more than one wife only when he is financially able to support this extra burden. The women's rights associations of Yemen have taken a wait-and-see attitude toward this victory, however, because although the law was passed by a majority of the parliamentary deputies, President Ali Abdullah al-Saleh has yet to put it into effect.

Perhaps Nujood does not realize this yet, but she has shattered a taboo. The news of her divorce traveled around the world, relayed by many international media, bringing an end to the silence enshrouding a practice that is unfortunately all too widespread in a number of other countries: Afghanistan, Egypt, India, Iran, Mali, Pakistan. . . . If her story touches us so deeply, however, it's also because it impels us to take a good look at ourselves. In the West, it's fashionable to instinctively bemoan the fate of Muslim women, yet conjugal violence and the practice of child marriage are hardly restricted to the Islamic world.

In Yemen, many factors drive fathers to marry off their daughters before they reach puberty. Husnia al-Kadri reminds us that "poverty, local customs, and a lack of education play a role." Family honor, the fear of adultery, the settling of scores between rival tribes—the reasons cited by the parents are many and various. Out in the countryside, adds al-Kadri, there is even a tribal proverb: "To guarantee a happy marriage, marry a nine-year-old girl."

For many people, sadly, child marriages are customary, even normal. Nadia al-Saqqaf, the editor in chief of the *Yemen Times*, told me recently that a girl of nine married to a Saudi man died three days after her wedding. Instead of demanding an investigation of this scandalous situation, her parents hastened to apologize to the husband, as if trying to make amends for defective merchandise, and even offered him, in exchange, the dead child's seven-year-old sister. Nujood's rebellion, honorable in our eyes, is moreover considered by conservatives as an outrageous affront, punishable, according to extremists, by a murderous "honor crime."

After the glitz and glitter of New York, the everyday reality of our little Yemeni heroine is still far, unfortunately, from the pleasant world of fairy tales.

It was Nujood's wish to return to live with her parents. Nujood's family has broken off all ties with her former husband, and no one knows where he is. At home, her older brothers resent the international attention aroused by her divorce. The neighbors complain about the comings and goings of foreign television crews. And not all the many people who come to hear her story are well-intentioned.

Shada as well is not beyond the reach of threats and danger. Her detractors accuse her of promoting a negative image of Yemen. Meanwhile, out in the countryside, nongovernmental organizations are attempting to educate the rural population about the problems linked to early marriage, while remaining sensitive to local traditions. For example, Oxfam, the organization that is by far the most invested in this project, must weigh its words carefully when it organizes consciousness-raising workshops in the southern part of the country. Instead of discussing "the legal age of marriage," Oxfam prefers to talk about a "safe age," emphasizing the risks linked to child marriage: psychological trauma, death in childbirth, dropping out of school. The task remains a difficult one, however. "Several of our colleagues who work out in the field have already become the objects of fatwas issued by the local sheikhs, who accuse them of promoting Western decadence and not respecting Islam," says Souha Bashren, the special projects manager at Oxfam. It would seem that the path to a more enlightened future is a long and tortuous one.

In Nujood's neighborhood, the lights don't shine the way they do in New York. In the winter it's cold, and heating a home is expensive. In Sana'a, the long evening gowns remain behind their shop windows. Every morning someone must go buy bread for the whole family. Often the alarm clock fails to ring, and Nujood's big brothers doze until midday. As for her father, who is ill and sometimes feverish, he has not yet found work. Nujood's mother increasingly forgets to attend to even the slightest household chores.

Overwhelmed by the stress of family troubles, Nujood and her younger sister Haïfa had to withdraw from their neighborhood school. After a difficult period, however, both girls are now preparing to attend a private school that offers a more supportive educational environment. The royalties from Nujood's book, which is being translated into sixteen languages, have already begun helping finance the girls' schooling and contributing to the support of the family, paying for food, rent, school supplies, and clothing for the children. Later, the money will help Nujood pursue her desire to become a lawyer and to establish a foundation to assist young girls in difficulties. A generous soul, Nujood also dreams of someday building a proper house for her whole family.

Whenever I travel to Sana'a, she asks me to bring her colored pencils. Crouching on the floor of the modest living room, she always draws the same colorful building with plenty of windows. One day, I asked her if it was a house, a school, or a boarding school.

"It's the house of joy," she replied with a big smile. "The house of happy little girls."

DELPHINE MINOUI
SEPTEMBER 2009

Acknowledgments

We would like to thank warmly all those men and women who opened their doors to us, allowing us to tell Nujood's story so that she can be an example to other girls and encourage them to demand their rights.

We would particularly like to thank Shada Nasser, Nujood's lawyer, as well as the judges of the court in Sana'a: Judge Mohammad al-Ghazi, Judge Abdo, and Judge Abdel Wahed.

A big thank-you to the entire staff of the *Yemen Times*, and especially to their editor in chief, Nadia Abdulaziz al-Saqqaf, and to their former reporter, Hamed Thabet, who is currently serving as the political advisor to the German Embassy in Sana'a.

We are infinitely grateful to Husnia al-Kadri, director of women's affairs at the University of Sana'a, who helped us with her research into the question of early marriage in Yemen.

Our conversations with the personnel of Oxfam,

and with Wameedh Shakir and Souha Bashren in particular, were also of great assistance to us.

Thanks are owed to Njala Matri, the principal of the local school in the Sana'a neighborhood of Rawdha, who allowed Nujood to return to the classroom and continue her studies.

We would like to express our profound gratitude to Eman Mashour, without whom this book would never have been published. Her support for the cause of women's rights in Yemen, her patience, and her talents as a translator were of considerable help to us.

From the bottom of our hearts, we thank Borzou Daragahi for his moral support and his enthusiasm for the writing of this book.

Hyam Yared, Martine Minoui, and Chloé Radiguet kindly agreed to be the first readers of these pages. Thank you for your help!

And finally, we are infinitely indebted to Ellen Knickmeyer, who brought us together in the first place.

This book is dedicated to Arwa, Rym, and all the little Yemeni girls who dream of freedom.

DELPHINE MINOUI and NUJOOD ALI

Notes

Delphine Minou has supplied notes for the conven-
ience of the reader; a few translator's notes have been
added where appropriate for this American edition.

10 *culture of khat*
When chewed, the leaves of the khat plant produce an effect of euphoria that allows the user to
forget hunger and fatigue. Other side effects include emotional instability, manic behavior, and
hallucinations, while withdrawal symptoms can
range from irritability to lethargy and depres-
sion. The World Health Organization has classi-
fied khat as a drug of abuse that can produce
psychological dependence, and although it has
been outlawed in many countries, this narcotic is
sold freely in Yemen. Its consumption, predomi-
nantly by men, is a time-honored social ritual so
widespread that khat has become the country's
main agricultural product, absorbing more than
two thirds of the nation's annual water resources
in a country facing a serious threat of water short-
ages in the near future. —Translator's note

13 niqabs *that match their long black robes*
The *niqab* is a veil that covers the face, allowing only the eyes to be seen. It is worn most commonly by Muslim women in the Arab countries of the Persian Gulf—Yemen, Saudi Arabia, Bahrain, Qatar, Kuwait, and Oman—and is also common in Turkey, Pakistan, and Iraq.

24 *two months and four years*
Yemen has one of the highest rates of infant mortality and maternal deaths during childbirth in the world.

31 *real rhinoceros horn*
Since the *jambia* handle often indicates the social status of the wearer, daggers made with real—and necessarily smuggled—rhinoceros horn and elephant ivory are much more prized than ones with handles of ordinary bone or horn. —Translator's note

36 *object of child trafficking*
The trafficking of Yemeni children in Saudi Arabia is a plague affecting all disadvantaged youngsters who do not go to school. Some local nongovernmental organizations estimate that thirty percent of the school-age children living near the border with Saudi Arabia leave each year to try their luck in their northern neighbor, where work conditions are appalling, and although the subject is taboo in

Yemeni families, cases of sexual abuse have been recorded.

39 *the tradition of* sighar
Still rather widespread in rural and poor urban areas, the ancient custom of *sighar*, or "marriage exchange," involves giving a younger sister of the groom to a member of his bride's family as a dowry. In Yemen, dowries have great social and economic importance, and are customarily negotiated before a wedding by the men of both families.

44 *legal age of fifteen*
In 1999, it became legal in Yemen for parents to give their daughters in marriage before the age of fifteen, provided that the husband promises not to touch his wife until she has reached puberty—a provision so vague that it welcomes arbitrary interpretations and is rarely respected.

54 *"Too young? When the prophet . . ."*
The reference to the marriage of the Prophet reflects widespread misunderstanding of the fact, as pointed out by scholars, that the marriage between Mohammad and Aïsha ("Mother of the Faithful") was God's wish.

65 *the Houthi rebels*
In 2004, Hussein Badreddin al-Houthi, a leader of the minority Zaidi sect of Shiite Islam, began a

bloody rebellion in northern Yemen and around Sana'a in an attempt to overthrow President Ali Abdullah al-Saleh, break Yemen's ties to the United States, and restore the Shiite imamate that was toppled in 1962. The rebels, currently led by Abdul-Malik al-Houthi, appear to control much of Sa'ada Province, on the northwestern border with Saudi Arabia, and recent fighting between the army and Houthi forces has destroyed entire villages, left thousands dead, and driven tens of thousands from their homes. —Translator's note

67 *the black veils usually worn*

According to local lore in Sana'a, women began to veil themselves in black when the Imam Yahya seized power in northern Yemen following the demise of the Ottoman Empire. Imam Yahya sought to establish a stable, modern state, but was himself assassinated in an attempted coup in February 1948. —Translator's note

79 *who fights for women's rights*

In 1999, Shada Nasser achieved notoriety with her defense of Amina Ali Abduladif, married at the age of ten and condemned to death by a Yemeni court after being convicted of killing her husband. Due to an unprecedented public outcry, the capital sentence was finally suspended in 2005. Amina was at last released, after spending some ten years behind bars, but she lives in hiding, fearing the vengeance of her in-laws.

157   *the army checkpoint*
Al Qaeda has a growing presence in Yemen, and the authorities have increased security measures, especially on the road to the airport. In a worsening crisis, the Yemeni government now battles three insurgencies: the Houthi rebels in the north, Al Qaeda terrorists seeking to establish a regional base in the country, and a southern secessionist movement fighting under the banner of the formerly independent South Yemen. —Translator's note

170 *her self-confidence*
Delphine Minoui, "Nojoud, 10 ans, divorcée au Yemen," *Le Figaro*, June 24, 2008.

171   *before the age of eighteen*
Early Marriage in Yemen: A Base Line Story to Combat Early Marriage in Hadramout and Hadeyda Governates, Sana'a University, 2006. According to this study, early marriages are the main reason why Yemeni girls lack access to education. In Yemen, seventy percent of women are illiterate.

Reading Group Guide

1. Honor is obviously very important to the men of Nujood's family. What does the notion of honor mean in rural Yemeni culture, and how does it differ from Western ideas of honor? When Nujood, Shada, and their allies go to court to seek a divorce for Nujood, what conception of honor are *they* defending?

2. Nujood mentions a tribal proverb that says "To guarantee a happy marriage, marry a nine-year-old girl." How does this traditional view of a "happy marriage" differ from the Western view? Are there any ways in which they might be similar?

3. Nujood says that when her family was driven from Khardji, they lost "a small corner of paradise." How do the injustices endured by Nujood's father and brother, Fares, show that life in a patriarchal society can be hard not just for women, but for male Yemenis, too?

Consider how the actions of Omma, Mona, Nujood's mother-in-law, Dowla, and Shada reflect differences in

their life experiences, personalities, backgrounds, and re-
lationships with Nujood. For example:

4. What do you think Omma was thinking when Nujood
told her about the abuse? Can you understand her lack of
action?

5. Conversely, why was Dowla willing and able to give
Nujood the help and advice that no one else was willing
to provide?

6. Were you surprised when one of Nujood's primary op-
pressors turned out to be a woman? Nujood's mother-in-
law is a strong personality who treats the young girl
harshly and fails to come to her defense on her wedding
night. How does this play, paradoxically, into the idea of
Yemen as a highly patriarchal society? Do you see any
similarity, for example, between the mother-in-law's behavior and the fact that in some African societies, it is the
women who enforce the practice of female circumcision?

7. How do you interpret the behavior of Mona, not only
in her attempts to protect Nujood, but in her difficult re-
lationship with her older sister, Jamila?

8. What enables Shada to take up Nujood's cause so
quickly and effectively? How does Shada, whom Nujood
calls her "second mother," open up Nujood's world? Who
else teaches Nujood about what a "real" family can be like?

9. The urban elites Nujood encounters in the courtroom and at the *Yemen Times* lead very different lives from those of Nujood and the country people of Yemen. How are these "enlightened" people actually disconnected from the rest of their society? For example, Nujood tells us several times that child marriage is common in Yemen, so why did the judges seem so shocked by Nujood's tender age? Do you think they were unaware of their society's problem with early marriage, or were they simply blind to the real-life consequences for girls like Nujood? Was there something special about Nujood that prompted the judges to help her, or was she simply the first girl who had come to them asking for a divorce?

10. Shada and Nujood chose the less "elitist" option for Nujood's schooling. Do you think Nujood made the right decision—to stay in Yemen for her education? Do you think she will become a lawyer and help other girls like herself, as she says she hopes to do? Closer to home, Nujood talks about her protective feelings toward her sisters Mona and Haïfa, and even toward her big brother Fares. Do you think Nujood will be able to protect her siblings? What might stand in her way?

11. How has the international publicity surrounding the divorce affected Nujood's family and community? Has it enlightened her relatives and neighbors? Or do you think it may have caused dissension within the family and alienated them from their own society?

12. Khat plays a small but sinister role in Nujood's story. Khat is illegal in the United States, but some people in immigrant communities compare it to coffee and support its important traditional role in social situations. U.S. authorities counter that it is more like cocaine than coffee. After reading this book, what effect do you think khat has on its users and on Yemen in general? Do you feel that it contributed to Nujood's father's problems? If so, how? How do you think its use and effects might compare to social drugs in the United States? And most important, what does it tell us about *any* society that devotes so much of its valuable resources to tuning out from itself, so to speak?

Girls Like Nujood Need Our Help

The Girls World Communication Center (GWCC), a nongovernmental organization based in Sana'a, recently launched a new program called ENTELAK. This program helps girls who have been forced to leave school and those who are young victims of early marriage to continue their educations.

Local GWCC members assist the girls in their studies, helping them to secure a good future. They also lead campaigns to raise awareness among the girls' families and communities about the importance of educating women.

Founded in 1998, GWCC was the first language center in Yemen catering exclusively to girls. Its programs have since expanded to include skills and leadership training, scholarships, and networking opportunities. Supporters include the British Council, the United Nations Development Fund for Women (UNIFEM), and the *Glamour* Women of the Year Fund. If you wish to make a donation, you can access the website at **http://www.yldf.org/** or contact **gwcc@yldf.org**.

READ IT FIRST. PASS IT ON.

READ IT FORWARD

Sign up for our
monthly newsletter at

ReadItForward.com

http://www.readitforward.com
for great reading recommendations,
downloadable reader's guides,
author chats, sneak peeks at
future publications, and fabulous
book giveaways.